Better Homes and Gardens®

100 crafts under $10

Better Homes and Gardens® Books
Des Moines, Iowa

Better Homes and Gardens® Books
An imprint of Meredith® Books

100 crafts under $10

Editor: Carol Field Dahlstrom
Writer: Susan M. Banker
Designer: Catherine Brett
Technical Assistant: Judy Bailey
Copy Chief: Terri Fredrickson
Copy and Production Editor: Victoria Forlini
Editorial Operations Manager: Karen Schirm
Managers, Book Production: Pam Kvitne, Marjorie J. Schenkelberg, Rick von Holdt
Contributing Copy Editor: Arianna McKinney
Contributing Proofreaders: Jessica Kearney Heidgerken, Heidi Johnson, Jeanée Ledoux
Photographers: Peter Krumhardt, Scott Little, Andy Lyons Cameraworks
Technical Illustrator: Shawn Drafahl
Electronic Production Coordinator: Paula Forest
Editorial and Design Assistants: Kaye Chabot, Mary Lee Gavin, Karen McFadden

Meredith® Books
Publisher and Editor in Chief: Linda Raglan Cunningham
Design Director: Matt Strelecki
Executive Editor, Food and Crafts: Jennifer Dorland Darling

Publisher: James D. Blume
Executive Director, Marketing: Jeffrey Myers
Executive Director, New Business Development: Todd M. Davis
Executive Director, Sales: Ken Zagor
Director, Operations: George A. Susral
Director, Production: Douglas M. Johnston
Business Director: Jim Leonard

Vice President and General Manager: Douglas J. Guendel

***Better Homes and Gardens*® Magazine**
Editor in Chief: Karol DeWulf Nickell

Meredith Publishing Group
President, Publishing Group: Stephen M. Lacy
Vice President-Publishing Director: Bob Mate

Meredith Corporation
Chairman and Chief Executive Officer: William T. Kerr

In Memoriam: E. T. Meredith III (1933–2003)

All of us at Better Homes and Gardens® Books are dedicated to providing you with information and ideas to create beautiful and useful projects. We welcome your comments and suggestions. Write to us at: Better Homes and Gardens Books, Crafts Editorial Department, 1716 Locust Street—LN112, Des Moines, IA 50309-3023.

If you would like to purchase any of our crafts, cooking, gardening, home improvement, or home decorating and design books, check wherever quality books are sold. Or visit us at: bhgbooks.com

It doesn't have to cost much money

No matter how much or little money we have, it is satisfying to be thrifty. We all love to craft, and it doesn't have to take a lot of money to make a special gift or a decoration for your home. Of course, we all have times when new crafting products excite us so much that we buy them all just to try them!

But it really doesn't take expensive products to create exquisite crafts. In this book we'll show you 100 wonderful projects you can make for very little money.

When we chose the projects for this book, we assumed that, as a clever crafting person, you have a few supplies on hand. We know that you have scissors, glue, pencils, and paper, so we didn't include these in the total cost of making a project. And while we're sure many of you have some of the other items needed, we tried to make the total cost reflect items beyond the basics you would need to buy. We think you'll be amazed to see what beautiful and unique projects you can make for so little money.

Enjoy crafting and feeling so cleverly thrifty at the same time!

Carol Field Dahlstrom

contents

autumn

Leaves, candy corn, pumpkins, and more await in this project-packed chapter. Whether you love to paint, sew, or assemble things, encounter wonderful ways to be creative when capturing the beauty of the autumn season.

winter

From jolly Christmas surprises to sentimental Valentine's Day gifts, this chapter inspires everyone to make the holidays bright. Find painted jars, handmade soaps, and last-minute ornaments in this crafting collection that celebrates winter.

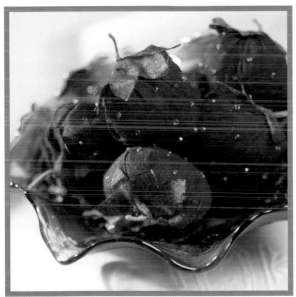

spring

Flowers bloom aplenty in this fresh-as-a-garden chapter. Learn how to make daisy May baskets, pansy serving trays, and beaded posy totes. More than 20 projects—from those for baby's room to dainty Easter eggs—help you to welcome spring.

summer

Whatever your style—seashore simple or country quaint, colorfully contemporary or primarily patriotic—find projects to make and love right here. Decoupage a set of bowls, decorate a denim purse, or paint a nifty clock—all in the name of summer.

Capture the beauty of autumn with crafts that celebrate the season. Discover dozens of ideas that are easy on the pocketbook, yet rich with designer flair. From earthy coasters that resemble fallen leaves to pretty painted pumpkins, you'll fall in love with the projects in this chapter.

autumn

1 pretty purse

Create a purse to coordinate with any outfit using a lovely fabric napkin or place mat.

what you'll need

14×20-inch fabric place mat or 20×20-inch fabric napkin

Scissors; needle and thread; sewing machine

Iron; 1 yard of satin cord or metal chain

Button or jewelry pin

here's how

1 Trim off the hem from the place mat or napkin. Fold the fabric in half lengthwise with right sides facing. Stitch lengthwise with ½-inch seam allowance. Press the seam open.

2 Center the seam of the tube and stitch across one end. Trim the corners and turn to right side. Fold the fabric piece in half lengthwise away from the seam and stitch through all layers at raw edge.

3 Turn to form a point for front flap.

4 Fold up bottom edge 6 to 7 inches depending on size of napkin or place mat; topstitch side seams close to edge and along point of flap. Stitch cord or chain handle at sides of purse. Sew on a button or attach a jewelry pin to the flap.

total cost

place mat or napkin	$1.99
cord or chain	2.00
button or pin	.50
total	$4.49

② leaf coasters

Bring a sense of the season to the table with photocopies of pressed leaves.

what you'll need
Pressed leaves
Paper; glue stick
Color photocopier
Heavy paper
Scissors
Thick white crafts glue

total cost

paper	$ .50
photocopies	2.00
total	**$2.50**

here's how
1 Arrange pressed leaves of different shapes and colors on a sheet of paper, leaving a bit of space between them. Use a glue stick to secure the leaves to the paper. Make color copies of the sheet on heavy paper.
2 Cut out the leaves. Arrange the leaves as desired, using crafts glue to secure them to one another.

③ autumn wreath

Bronze a bounty of leaves, pods, and other pickings to make a spectacular front door wreath.

total cost

wreath	$2.29
dried items	3.59
spray paint	1.89
wire	.40
total	**$8.17**

what you'll need
Newspapers
Grapevine wreath
Dried pods, pinecones, leaves, moss, and other natural items
Bronze or copper spray paint; hot-glue gun and glue sticks
Silver crafting wire; wire cutters; ½-inch dowel

here's how
1 In a well-ventilated work area, cover work surface with newspapers. Place wreath and natural dried items (except for moss) on newspaper and spray with paint. Let the paint dry. Turn the items over and spray again with paint. Let dry.
2 Hot-glue moss to one side of the wreath. Arrange and glue remaining items in place.
3 Cut 24-inch lengths of wire. Wrap randomly around wreath leaving long tails; twist to secure. Wind tails around a dowel to shape.

④ sachet ball

The sweet scent of roses will linger throughout autumn with this ribbon-wrapped sachet.

what you'll need
Small balloon
Fabric stiffening medium
Approximately 6 yards of assorted sheer silk or polyester ribbons for ribbon embroidery in ¼- and ⅜-inch widths
1 to 2 cups of dried rosebuds and petals; needle and thread
3 decorative buttons

total cost

balloon	$ .10
fabric stiffening medium	1.99
ribbon	3.00
dried rosebuds and petals	1.00
decorative buttons	1.00
total	$7.09

here's how
1 Inflate balloon to 3½-inch diameter and spray with stiffening medium while wrapping layers of ribbon randomly around the balloon. Continue with layers of ribbon and stiffening medium to desired thickness, leaving spaces between ribbon that are small enough to keep petals inside.
2 Hang balloon and allow to dry completely. When dry, cut balloon and remove.
3 Fill ribbon sachet with rosebuds and petals. Gather around top edge to close. Attach loops and tails of ribbon for bow, threading on buttons as desired. Make ribbon loop for hanging.

⑤ autumn edging

Frame photos, souvenir postcards, special greeting cards, and more with fresh herbs that dry while in place.

what you'll need
Fresh or dried thyme
Paddle wire (available in crafts and floral supply stores)
Wire cutters
Wood picture frame

here's how
1 Assemble 3- to 4-inch-long sprigs of fresh or dried thyme into bundles of 8 to 10 sprigs each; wrap the stems with paddle wire.
2 Place one bundle on the frame so it extends just beyond the corner. Arrange a second bundle over the stems of the first and wrap wire around stems and frame. Continue all the way around until the frame is covered.

total cost

herbs	$2.50
wire	1.79
frame	2.00
total	$6.29

6 wired candles

Banish autumn darkness with the warm glow of candlelight.

what you'll need
Drill and bits; 18-gauge wire
3-inch-thick pieces of wood or logs
Strong adhesive, such as E6000
Wire cutters; dripless taper candles

here's how
1 Using a drill bit to fit wire, drill an off-center hole in each wood piece.
2 Cut an 18-inch-long piece of wire for each candle. Glue one end of the wire into the hole. Let the glue dry.
3 Wrap wire around candle. Shape wire end into a curlicue.

Note: Never leave burning candles unattended.

total cost

wire	$2.00
wood	.50
candles	4.00
total	$6.50

pinstriped
pumpkin ⑦

For indoor fall decorating, paint pumpkins with a classic country motif.

what you'll need
Newspapers
Pumpkin
Latex primer
Paintbrushes, including a narrow, flat artist's brush
Acrylic or latex paints in ivory and ocher or mustard yellow
Soft cloth
Antiquing stain

here's how
1 In a well-ventilated work area, cover the work surface with newspapers. Spray or paint the pumpkin with primer. Let the primer dry.
2 Paint the pumpkin yellow. Apply two coats if necessary to achieve good coverage and a deep color. Let the paint dry.
3 Use a narrow, flat artist's paintbrush to paint three ivory rings around the pumpkin. Let the paint dry.
4 Use a soft cloth to apply a thin coat of antiquing stain to the pumpkin, wiping off the excess. Let the stain dry.

total cost

pumpkin	$2.50
primer	1.00
paint	3.00
stain	2.59
total	$9.09

⑧ halloween basket

When excited trick-or-treaters come to call, serve ghoulish treats in an orange and black bead-trimmed basket.

total cost

basket	$2.99
beaded trim	2.49
napkins	1.98
total	$7.46

what you'll need
Hot-glue gun and glue sticks
Beaded trim in orange and black
Large, square wicker basket
2 orange and black plaid fabric napkins

here's how
1 Working in short sections, hot-glue beaded trim around the outside rim of the basket.
2 To line the basket, fold napkins in half lengthwise. Place one napkin inside the basket, fitting each end to just inside the top of the outer rim. Smooth the middle section down inside basket to fit into corners. Hot-glue the napkin in place. Repeat with the second napkin, placing it on the opposite sides of the basket. Let dry.

⑨ bittersweet pumpkin

A simply carved
pumpkin makes
an elegant holder
for lush
autumn foliage.

what you'll need
Pumpkin
Knife
Spoon
Sprigs of bittersweet

here's how
1 Cut the pumpkin neatly in half horizontally. Using a spoon,
  scrape out the insides.
2 Cut upside-down V shapes out of the top half. Leave enough
  space between Vs so the top sits stably on the bottom.
3 Poke bittersweet into the openings of the pumpkin.

total cost

pumpkin	$2.50
bittersweet	2.00
total	$4.50

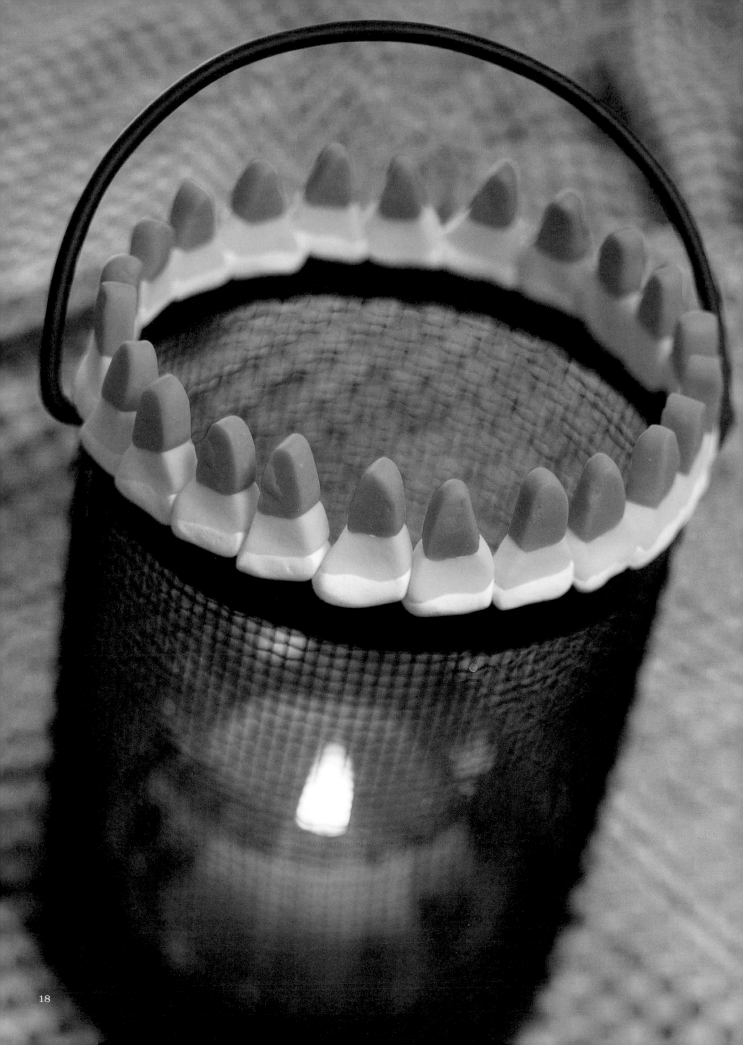

10 candy corn baskets

Bands of clay candy corn adorn wire baskets for use as candleholders or as treat dishes for little tricksters.

what you'll need
Polymer clay, such as Sculpey, in
  white, yellow, and orange
Crafts knife
Black wire basket or bowl

total cost

clay	$4.50
basket or bowl	3.25
total	$7.75

here's how

1 Work the clay in your hands to make it warm and pliable. Roll each color of clay into a long rope. The white clay should be approximately ½-inch wide, and the yellow and orange clay should be slightly thinner.

2 Gently flatten both the white and the yellow ropes by pressing your finger down the length of each rope.

3 Place the yellow rope on top of the white, joining them with slight pressure. Pinch the top of the orange rope to make it triangular in shape; then press the flat bottom on top of the yellow rope.

4 Cut ¼-inch slices off the finished roll. Each slice needs to be smoothed and finished by pinching the outside edges with your fingertips to look like candy corn. Firmly press the white bottom of the finished candy corn onto the rim of the container. Bake the clay-topped basket or bowl according to the clay manufacturer's directions.

⑪potion goblets

For a Halloween toast, raise these festive flutes filled with your favorite potion.

what you'll need
Clear glasses with long stems
Pipe cleaners in purple, orange, black, and lime green
Silver adhesive stars

here's how
1 Wash and dry the glasses. Begin at the bottom of the glass stem and wrap it tightly with a purple pipe cleaner. Continue wrapping the stem using the pipe cleaners as shown, *above*. When wrapping the top lime green pipe cleaner, wrap half of the length and then form the end into a spiral or zigzag shape.
2 Apply stars randomly to the outside of the glass top, avoiding the rim area. Remove the trims before washing the glass.

total cost

glasses	$4.00
pipe cleaners	1.59
stars	.50
total	$6.09

12 boo-tiful jar toppers

Mold simple Halloween shapes from clay to put a spook-tacular spell on treat jars.

what you'll need
Rolling pin
Polymer clay, such as Sculpey, in green, white, black, orange, and purple
Pinking shears or biscuit cutter
Small jars with lids
Glass baking dish
Scissors
Unserrated table knife
Strong adhesive, such as E6000

total cost

clay	$3.50
jars	2.00
total	$5.50

here's how
1 Roll out green clay to ³⁄₁₆ inch thick. Cut into a circle with pinking shears or a biscuit cutter to fit the size of the lid. Place the clay piece on the baking dish.
2 To shape the ghost, roll out a smooth flat piece of white clay to about ³⁄₁₆-inch thick. Use scissors to cut clay into a square. Form a ghost shape from white clay and drape the square piece over it. Trim the edges if needed to fit on the lid. Roll small circles from black clay and press onto the face to make the eyes and mouth.

3 To form a pumpkin, roll orange clay into a ball, pressing down to make a squatty pumpkin or pinching the top to make a tall one. Use a knife to press in vertical lines. Form a green clay stem and a narrow green coil to make a vine. Press onto pumpkin.
4 Roll small balls of purple clay to place at the base of the pumpkin. Place clay pieces on the glass baking dish. Bake in the oven according to the clay manufacturer's instructions. Let cool.
5 Glue clay pieces together as shown, *left*. Glue green bases to tops of lids. Let the glue dry.

haunted (13) centerpiece

Paint and glitter leave their fiendish marks on flea market finds for an eerie grouping.

what you'll need
Old vases, candleholders, ornamental tray and picture frames, metal bowl with handles, chain, and other desired pieces
Newspapers
Spray paints in black and pewter
Plastic canvas, optional
White glue; paintbrush
Glitter in black and silver
Silver candles; dry ice and dried roses, optional

here's how
1 In a well-ventilated work area, place items to be painted on newspapers. Spray paint the items black. If painting a frame such as the oval one, *left,* first remove the glass. Paint one side of the glass. Let it dry. Spray the items with pewter paint, allowing some of the black to show through. Let dry.
2 Reassemble the frame. Note: The one shown here has a pattern in the center created by the plastic backing showing through the glass. If your frame does not have this type of backing, cut and insert a piece of plastic canvas to achieve the effect.
3 Thin glue with water and paint on the areas where glitter is desired. Sprinkle black and silver glitters onto the glue. Let dry. Shake off the excess.
4 Arrange the items on the tray. Place candles in candleholders. Place roses in vase if desired. Add dry ice if desired.

Note: Dry ice can cause severe burns. Always wear gloves when handling dry ice and keep it out of the reach of children. Also never leave burning candles unattended.

total cost

flea market finds	$2.80
spray paints	3.98
glitter	1.50
candles	1.50
total	**$9.78**

(14) pumpkin mats

Mealtime will be safe from uninvited specters when guarded by jack-o'-lantern place mats and coasters recycled from grocery sacks.

what you'll need
Brown paper grocery sack
Scissors
Acrylic paints in orange and green
Disposable plate; paintbrush
Foam pumpkin stamp in two sizes
Decorative-edge scissors
Compass
2 yards of green jumbo rickrack
Sewing machine

here's how
1 For the place mat, cut off the bottom of the sack. Cut off the seam. Fold the sack in half and trim to desired size. Press the folded sack flat.
2 Put small amounts of paint on the plate. Paint the pumpkin parts of the stamps orange and the stems green. Stamp the pumpkins on the place mat. Continue stamping pumpkins in this manner until you achieve the desired look. Let the paint dry.
3 Trim the open ends of the sack with decorative-edge scissors. Machine-stitch rickrack around the edges of the place mat.
4 For the coaster, use the compass to draw two 4-inch circles on a sack scrap. Cut out the circles. Place the circles together and machine-stitch around the edges to secure the layers. Stamp a pumpkin in the center. Trim the edges with decorative-edge scissors.

total cost

paints	$2.00
stamps	2.00
rickrack	1.59
total	$5.59

⑮mini pumpkin topiary

Welcome autumn visitors with an arrangement that takes advantage of the season.

what you'll need
Wire coat hanger
Wire cutters
3 miniature pumpkins in graduated sizes
Hot-glue gun and glue sticks
Sea sponge or cellulose sponge
Green acrylic paint
Small terra-cotta pot
Crafts foam; U-pins
Fresh autumn leaves
Raffia; bittersweet

here's how
1 Cut two 2-inch pieces of wire from a coat hanger as shown in Photo A, *left*.
2 Insert one end of a piece of wire into or beside the stem of the largest pumpkin. Place a drop of glue where the wire enters the pumpkin as shown in Photo B.
3 Insert the other end of the wire into the bottom of the middle pumpkin as shown in Photo C.
4 Attach the smallest pumpkin to the middle pumpkin in the same manner.
5 Using the sea sponge, pat green paint onto the terra-cotta pot, allowing the clay color to show through. If desired, use a cellulose sponge by tearing away pieces from the surface to roughen it.
6 Fill the pot almost to the top with crafts foam. Pin a collar of leaves to the foam with U-pins. Insert a short piece of coat hanger wire into the bottom pumpkin; then push the other end into the crafts foam. Tie raffia in a bow around the rim of the pot and glue sprigs of bittersweet to the raffia.

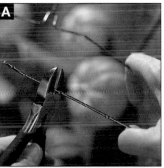

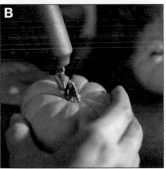

total cost

pumpkins	$1.00
paint	1.00
terra-cotta pot	.29
crafts foam	.15
U-pins	.30
bittersweet and raffia	.25
total	$2.99

(16) happy halloween pillow

Embroidery floss stitches lend charming detail to these vivid checkered and pumpkin pillows.

what you'll need for pumpkin pillow
Tracing paper; pencil
Scissors
Ruler
6½×6½-inch pieces of felt in lime green, orange, yellow, and black
⅓ yard of green felt
Pins
Needle
Cotton embroidery floss in orange, pink, and black
Fiberfill

here's how
1 Enlarge (200 percent) and trace the pumpkin pillow pattern, *opposite,* onto tracing paper and cut out. Cut one frame shape from lime green felt and two 12-inch squares from green. Cut pumpkin pieces from orange, yellow, and black felt.
2 Center the frame on one green square. Pin in place and stitch with straight stitches around the outside using orange floss and around the inside using pink. Use three plies of floss for all stitches. Use black floss to attach the features to the pumpkin. Make a French knot (see diagram, *below*) in the center of each eye. Pin the jack-o'-lantern inside the frame. Stitch around edges using black floss and straight stitches.

what you'll need for checkered pillow
Scissors; ruler
6×6-inch pieces of felt in black and orange
⅓ yard of camel felt; pins; needle
Cotton embroidery floss in purple
Fiberfill

total cost

felt for one pillow	$3.89
floss	.75
fiberfill	2.59
total	$7.23

French Knot

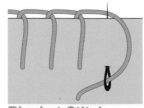

Blanket Stitch

ere's how
Cut four 6½×1½-inch strips each from orange and black felt. Cut
two 12-inch square pieces from camel felt.
Lay the orange strips side by side. Weave over and under using the
black strips. Center the square on one camel felt piece and pin in
place. Using three plies of purple floss and straight stitches, stitch
around the outside edges of the woven square.

nishing for either pillow
Pin the pillow front to the remaining 12-inch-square piece of felt.
Stitch the front to the back with blanket stitches (see diagram,
opposite) using coordinating floss. Leave a 10-inch opening on one
side. Stuff with fiberfill. Finish sewing the pillow edges together
with blanket stitches.

1 square = 1 inch
(enlarge 200%)

(17) hydrangea pumpkin

A cloud of hydrangea makes a beautiful presentation for the Halloween table when tucked into the top of a natural green and orange pumpkin.

total cost

pumpkin	$2.50
hydrangea	4.50
total	**$7.00**

what you'll need
Sharp knife
Medium or large pumpkin
Spoon
Scissors
Fresh-cut or artificial hydrangea
Plastic liner, optional

here's how
1 With the knife, cut a circle around the pumpkin stem. Scoop out the pumpkin using a spoon.
2 Use scissors to cut the hydrangea stems if needed to fit into the pumpkin. If using fresh-cut flowers, place a plastic liner in the pumpkin before arranging the flowers.

18 autumn pomanders

total cost

oranges	$3.20
cloves	1.25
total	**$4.45**

Fresh oranges and whole cloves are a winning combination for an autumn arrangement.

what you'll need
Embroidery needle
Oranges
Whole cloves

here's how
1 Using an embroidery needle, pierce the skin of each orange to make starter holes for the cloves. Outline monograms, lines, spirals, curlicues, or any design you wish.
2 Push a clove into each hole.

(19) pleasing plates

Edge mismatched plates and platters with the bounty of the season.

what you'll need

Dried flowers, pods, leaves, pinecones, twigs, or other natural items
Flea market plate or platter
Strong adhesive, such as E6000

here's how

1 Decide how to arrange the dried items on the plate or platter. Fill the entire border or create two small arrangements opposite each other. Use the photo, *opposite,* for ideas.
2 Glue the pieces in place, layering as desired. Let the glue dry.

total cost

dried items	$3.20
plate or platter	2.00
adhesive	1.69
total	$6.89

colored candleholders

For an informal gathering or a grand event, these vividly painted candleholders help brighten the celebration.

what you'll need
Newspapers
Wood candleholder; white spray primer
Acrylic paints in desired colors; paintbrush
Gems and clear adhesive or beading wire, wire cutters, beads, and pencil

here's how
1 In a well-ventilated work area, cover the work surface with newspapers. Place the candleholder in the center of the newspapers and spray on a light coat of primer. Let the primer dry. Spray on a second coat if needed. Let the primer dry.
2 Using the photos, *above* and *opposite,* for ideas, paint the entire piece the base color. Let the paint dry. Paint on accent colors; let dry.
3 For the gem-laden candleholder, glue the gems onto the candleholder using clear adhesive. Let the glue dry.
4 For the beaded candleholder, cut a length of wire approximately 12 inches long. Place a bead on one end and insert the wire through it several times. String beads on the wire until it is almost filled. Insert the end of the wire through the last bead several times. Wrap the beaded wire around the bottom of the candleholder, winding upward and looping the strand around twice to secure it. Coil the remaining ends of beaded wire around a pencil and shape as desired.

total cost

candleholder	$2.99
primer	1.89
paints	2.64
trims	2.19
total	$9.71

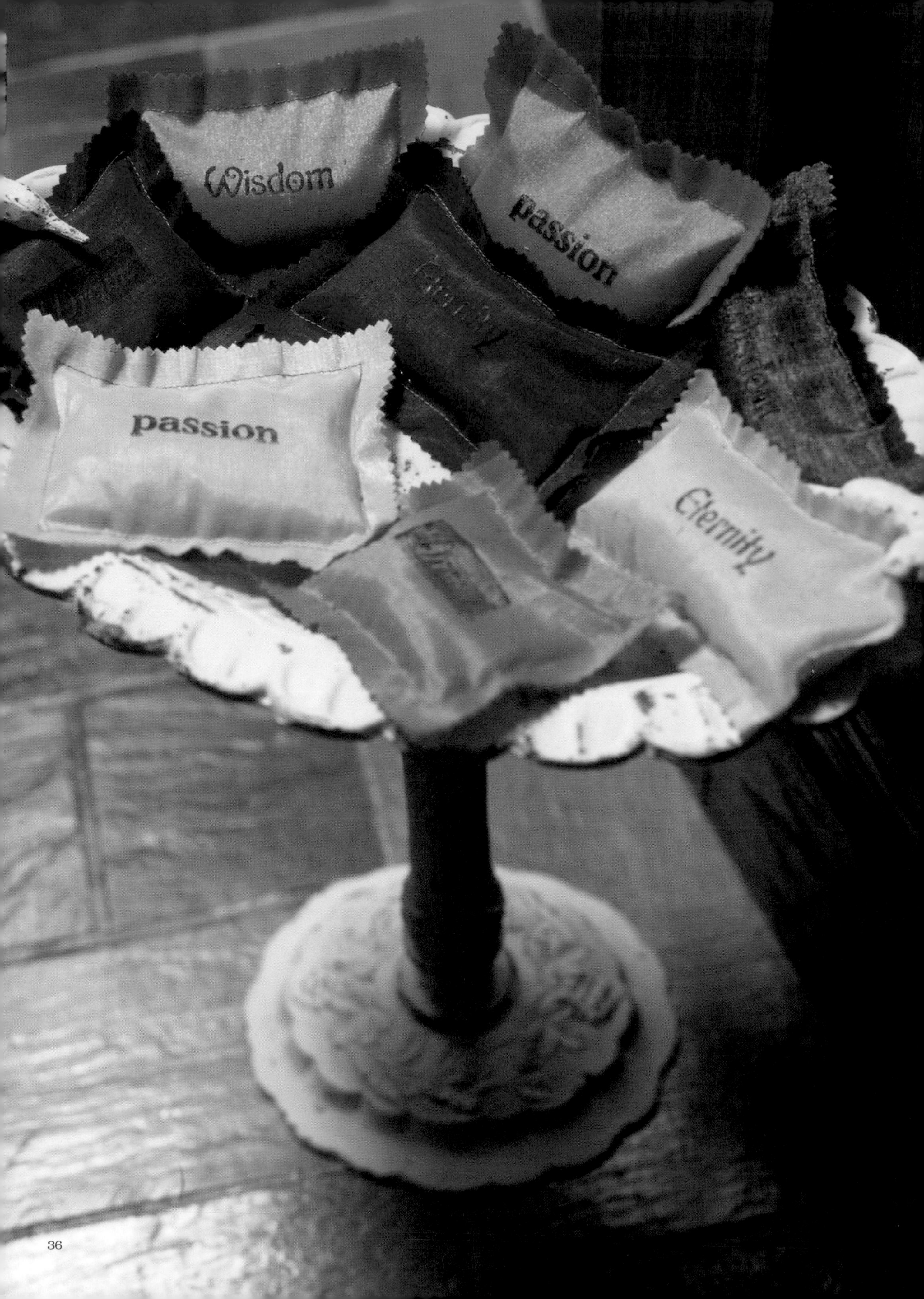
Wisdom
passion
passion
Eternity

㉑ stamped sachets

Stamped with symbolic words of life, these fabric sachets hold your favorite scents.

what you'll need
1 cup rice; zipper-lock plastic bag
Scented oil, such as lavender
    or seaside
Paper grocery sacks
Cookie sheet
Paintbrush
Black acrylic paint
Rubber word stamp, such as eternity,
    wisdom, love, dream, or passion
Two 5×7-inch pieces of cotton lamé
Matching thread
Fabric scrap, optional
Scissors; needle or sewing machine
Pinking shears

total cost

rice	$ .62
oil	1.99
paint	1.00
lamé	.50
stamp	4.99
total	$9.10

here's how
1 Transfer the rice into a zipper-lock plastic bag. Pour a few drops of scented oil into the bag. Tightly seal the bag. Knead and shake the bag to distribute the oil in the rice.
2 Lay a grocery sack on a cookie sheet. Pour the scented rice on the sack and set it in the sun to dry. It may take several days for the rice to dry. Replace the sack every day until there is no trace of oil on the paper.
3 Brush a thin coat of black paint onto the rubber stamp and press it on one piece of lamé. You may choose to test print the stamp on scrap fabric before working on the cotton lamé. Wash and dry the stamp after one or two stampings before using again. Let the paint dry.
4 Stack and trim both fabric pieces into slightly smaller rectangles, making sure the stamped message falls in the center. Stack the pieces, message side up. Machine-stitch, using the matching thread, all four sides of the sachet together ½ inch inside the cut edge, leaving a 1-inch opening. Pour the scented rice into the opening. Hand- or machine-stitch the opening closed.
5 Trim the edges of the sachet with pinking shears.

22 cornucopia of seeds

Create a beautiful Thanksgiving centerpiece that displays the colors of fall.

what you'll need
Newspapers
Black spray paint, optional
Plastic foam balls, such as styrofoam
Thick white crafts glue
Seeds, such as split peas, red kidney beans, navy beans, black beans, and lentils
Cornucopia; bittersweet

here's how
1 If desired, in a well-ventilated work area, cover the surface with newspapers. Spray-paint the foam balls black. Let them dry.
2 Cover a small area of each ball with glue. Place beans on the glued area, trying to keep the beans in horizontal rows. Allow each section to dry before starting a new area.
3 Place the seed balls in the cornucopia, tucking in sprigs of bittersweet to fill.

total cost

foam balls	$1.89
seeds	3.20
cornucopia	2.19
bittersweet	1.00
total	$8.28

㉓ leaf-print linens

On your next
nature hike,
gather leaves
to decorate
table linens.

total cost

place mat and napkin	$3.49
paints	1.86
total	**$5.35**

what you'll need
Iron
Fabric place mat and napkin
Pliable green leaves
Paper
Acrylic or fabric paints
Disposable plate
Paintbrush

here's how
1 Iron the place mat and napkin.
2 Choose several smooth, flat leaves with interesting shapes.
3 Cover the work surface with paper. Put a small amount of each paint color on a plate. Paint the underside of the leaf. (This side will show more lines and details.) Before stamping onto fabric, practice stamping a few leaves onto paper. Use enough paint to get a clean shape and allow veins in the leaves to show.
4 Pick up the leaf and place it on the fabric with the paint side down. Place a piece of clean paper over it, pressing down on the leaf and paper. Avoid moving or sliding the leaf. Carefully lift off the paper and the leaf. Repeat until the desired look is achieved on both items. Let dry.

leaf lunch box

An ideal gift for a young scholar, this lunch box captures the flavor of fall.

what you'll need
Metal lunch box; newspapers
Spray primer
Acrylic paint in burgundy, rust,
    purple, leaf green, and copper
Paintbrush; pliable green leaf; paper

total cost

lunch box	$2.49
primer	1.89
paints	4.40
total	$8.78

here's how

1 Wash and dry the lunch box. In a well-ventilated work area, cover the surface with newspapers. Open up the lunch box and place it on a flat work surface. Spray the outside of the lunch box with primer. Let dry.

2 Using the photo, *above,* as a guide, paint the sections and hardware of the lunch box as desired. Let the paint dry. Paint stripes on the frame area on each side. Let dry.

3 Paint a leaf with copper paint. First press it onto a piece of paper to test the print. If necessary, put on more paint where needed. Press the leaf onto one side of the lunch box. Remove the leaf and repeat on the remaining side. Let dry.

25 golden gourds

Stacked on a glass cake plate, these autumn gourds sparkle with gilding.

what you'll need
Gourds in desired shapes and sizes
Newspapers
Metallic gold spray or acrylic paint and paintbrush
Glass pedestal cake plate

here's how
1 Wash and dry the gourds.
2 Cover the work surface with newspapers in a well-ventilated area. Paint the gourds using spray paint or acrylic paint and a paintbrush. Let the paint dry.
3 Stack and arrange the gourds on a cake plate.

total cost

gourds	$3.00
paint	2.00
plate	4.50
total	$9.50

44

Come in from the cold and snuggle up to a wonderland of projects that are as merry as Santa's favorite season. Discover charming valentines filled with affection, Christmas trims to deck the halls and give as gifts, and wintertime wonders to enliven your spirit with handmade magic.

winter

㉖ bright candles

Reflect the light
of the season
with dazzling
mirror
candleholders.

total cost

paint	$ .88
mirror	1.79
gems	1.29
candle	2.29
total	$6.25

what you'll need
Toothpicks; acrylic paint in desired color
Small beveled mirror
Round gems; thick white crafts glue
Candle

here's how
1 Break a toothpick in half. Dip the side of the toothpick into paint and lay it on the mirror edge, creating a line. Repeat this process around the mirror edge, crossing the lines as desired. Let the paint dry.
2 Glue gems randomly around the mirror edge. Let the glue dry. Place a candle in the center of the mirror.

Note: Never leave burning candles unattended.

⟨27⟩ lucky game jars

Store a collection of small game pieces in these glass jars topped with painted wood accents.

what you'll need
Jars with lids
Glass paints, such as Liquitex Glossies, in red, blue, olive green, yellow ocher, or other desired colors
Paintbrush
Wood heart or ball with flat side
Red and black acrylic paints
Soft cloth
Crackle medium
Wood beads; sandpaper
⅛-inch-wide red suede cord
Thick white crafts glue

total cost

jar	$ .50
paints	4.88
wood accent	.90
crackle medium	1.00
wood beads	.25
cord	.50
total	**$8.03**

here's how
1 Wash and dry the jars and lids. Avoid touching the areas to be painted.
2 Paint the jar lids as desired using glass paints. Paint the wooden ball or heart red. Let the paint dry.
3 To apply an antique finish to the lid, dilute black acrylic paint with water. Brush it onto the painted area and gently dab it off with a soft cloth, allowing the paint to remain in the crevices. Let the paint dry.
4 To achieve a crackle finish on the lid, paint the lid a base color. Let the paint dry. Paint two coats of crackle medium over the painted surface. Let it dry. Paint on the top color, following the manufacturer's instructions.
5 Tie painted wood beads onto a length of suede cord and wrap around the neck of a jar.
6 Lightly sand the heart or ball to achieve a worn effect. Glue the heart or flat side of the ball onto lid. Let the glue dry. Fill jars with game pieces.

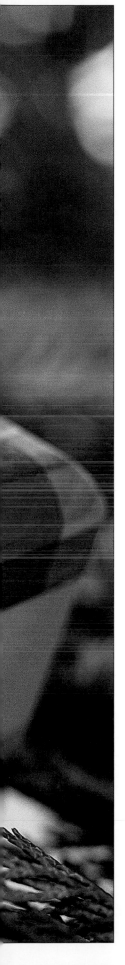

beribboned jewel box

Two layers of sheer ribbons create a lovely plaid top for this keepsake box.

what you'll need
Newspapers
4½×3×2½-inch hinged wood box
Spray acrylic sealer
Organza ribbons in a variety of widths in mauve, pink, tan, ivory, hunter green, and red
Scissors; disposable foam brush
Aluminum foil
Thick white crafts glue
Hot-glue gun and glue sticks
¼ yard moiré taffeta lining fabric, optional
½ yard of 1.4mm red variegated ribbon
Ruler
Red sewing thread and needle
3 artificial silver flower stamens

total cost

wood box	$3.99
acrylic sealer	1.79
ribbons	3.00
stamens	.29
total	$9.07

here's how

1 In a well-ventilated work area, cover work surface with newspapers. Spray the box inside and out with acrylic sealer. Set the box aside.

2 Plan the arrangement of organza ribbons for the plaid design with the bottom layer consisting of horizontal ribbons and the top layer of vertical ribbons.

3 Thin glue with water and brush on lid. When the glue begins to get tacky, apply the layer of horizontal ribbons over the lid, smoothing them from side to side. Let dry.

4 Apply thinned glue over the lid again. In the same manner apply the remaining ribbons from front to back. Also adhere a length of ribbon around all four sides of lid. Let dry.

5 Apply two more coats of thinned glue to the lid, letting the medium dry between coats. Prop the lid open with foil to prevent sealing it closed.

6 Glue a band of ribbon around each foot of the box. Apply a coat of thinned glue to the exterior box sides and bottom. Line the box with the taffeta fabric if desired.

7 For each flower, cut a 5½-inch-long piece of variegated ribbon. Work gathering stitches around three sides of the ribbon, leaving one long side ungathered. Pull the thread tightly to gather the stitches, coiling the ribbon around itself as you gather; secure with backstitches. Make three flowers.

8 Hot-glue stamens to the center of each flower. Tie two or three bows from the desired organza ribbons. Hot-glue the bows and flowers to the lid.

49

(29) holiday treat jar

This bright Christmas tree canister is perfect for holding the season's sweet surprises.

what you'll need

Glass jar with lid
Newspapers
Disposable plate
Glass paints, such as Liquitex Glossies, in dark green, white, purple, metallic gold, and other desired colors
Paintbrushes; toothpick
Old toothbrush

here's how

1 Wash the jar and let it dry. Avoid touching the areas to be painted.
2 Cover your work surface with newspapers. On the plate, place a small amount of paints. Pick up white and small amounts of green and purple on brush. Start to paint the snow at the bottom of the jar, using photo, *opposite,* as reference. Using the same colors (mostly green), paint a large tree on each side of the jar. Mix a small amount of purple with white and continue painting the top of the snow. Let the paint dry.
3 Using dark green, paint small trees around the jar between the large trees. Top each large tree with a star using metallic gold. Paint various sizes of gold stars on the lid. Let the paint dry.
4 To trim the large trees, dip the handle of a paintbrush into the desired colors of paint and dot on the trees. For garlands, use a toothpick and metallic gold paint. Make several dots in a row. Let the paint dry.
5 Dip the bristles of an old toothbrush into white paint. Run your finger along the bristles to splatter specks of paint over the jar to resemble snow. Let the paint dry.

total cost

jar	$1.99
paints	6.50
total	$8.49

holiday ③⓪
evergreen soap

Miniature
Christmas trees
make an
unexpected
appearance in
these pretty
holiday soaps.

what you'll need
Glycerin soap blocks in green and red
Knife; ruler
Plastic soap molds
Glass measuring cup

here's how
1 Slice a ½-inch-thick piece of green soap from the block. Trim the slice to measure a 2×1-inch rectangle. Using the knife, cut small triangles from the side until a tree shape is formed. Make as many trees as desired.
2 Arrange the tree shapes in the soap molds.
3 Break the red soap into small pieces and place into the measuring cup. Melt the red soap in the microwave or on the stove following the manufacturer's instructions. Allow to cool until a thin film appears over the top of the soap, about one minute. Gently skim the film aside and pour carefully into the molds. Let cool completely.
4 Remove the soaps from the molds.

total cost

¼ green soap block	$1.00
¼ red soap block	1.00
soap molds	2.99
total	$4.99

(31) kitchen tree

Tie a collection of vintage cookie cutters onto a tree-shape cooling rack for a quaint kitchen decoration.

total cost

cooling rack	$1.99
cookie cutters	5.00
ribbon	1.20
jingle bells	.75
narrow ribbon	.30
total	**$9.24**

what you'll need
8 cookie cutters in Christmas shapes
Cooling rack in tree shape
Scissors
4 yards of ⅜-inch-wide red plaid ribbon
Ruler
Three red jingle bells
⅛-inch green ribbon

here's how
1 Arrange the cookie cutters on the cooling rack.
2 Cut the red plaid ribbon into ½-yard pieces. Thread the ribbon through the back of the cooling rack and through each cookie cutter. Tie the ribbon ends into a bow.
3 Tie jingle bells to rack in same manner as for cookie cutters, using ⅛-inch green ribbon.

32 jeweled poinsettia

The Christmas tree lights glisten off this sparkling floral glass ornament.

what you'll need
Triangular glass ornament (available at crafts supply stores)
5 red teardrop rhinestones, each 1 inch long
2 diamond-shape green plastic mirror gems, each 1½ inches long
1 round gold rhinestone, ½ inch in diameter
Gem glue; 1 yard metallic gold cord

total cost

ornament	$1.99
rhinestones and gems	1.35
cord	.59
total	$3.93

here's how
1 Wash the glass ornament; let dry.
2 Arrange and glue the rhinestones and gems in the shape of a poinsettia as shown, *above*.
3 Glue gold trim around the edge of the ornament. Use cord to make a hanging loop and thread through the hole in the ornament. Let the glue dry.

silly snowmen

Make a whole clan of these cheery fellows in an evening, to trim the tree or dance around the house.

what you'll need
Toothpick
Thick white crafts glue
1- and 1½-inch foam balls, such as styrofoam
Oven-bake clay, such as Sculpey, in white, orange, and other desired colors
Rolling pin; pencil; scissors
Decorative-edge scissors; twigs
Glass baking dish
Paintbrush
White glitter

here's how
1 Coat one end of a toothpick with glue. Push it into a 1½-inch foam ball. Coat the exposed toothpick with glue. Push it into the 1-inch ball. Let the glue dry.
2 On a flat work surface, roll out white clay until it is ⅛ inch thick. Place the clay piece over the foam balls, shaping to form. Press the bottom flat.
3 Use a sharp pencil to press in eyes, a smile, nose, and buttons. Shape a tiny carrot from orange clay and press into the nose hole.
4 Using the photo, *below,* as inspiration, make clay hats and scarves as desired. To make a scarf, roll out the clay and cut the shape with scissors. Cut stripes with decorative-edge scissors. Place on the snowman.
5 Cut 2½-inch-long twigs for arms. Press a twig into each side of body. Bake on glass baking dish as directed by the manufacturer. Let cool.
6 Brush each snowman with water-thinned glue. Sprinkle glitter on the wet glue. Let dry.

total cost

foam balls	$ .50
clay	4.79
glitter	.50
total	$5.79

knitting
abbreviations
k = knit
p = purl
st(s) = stitch(es)
tog = together
rnd = round

34 knit-to-fit mittens

Like the little
kittens that were
smitten with their
mittens, these
kid-size
duplicate-stitch
versions are
purr-fectly suited to
your little ones.

what you'll need
Sizes 3 and 5 double-pointed knitting
  needles (dpn)
Lamb's Pride Superwash Bulky
  (100-gram or 110-yard skein) in
  desired color
Scissors; yarn needle
2 small stitch holders; stitch marker
10 yards of white yarn in a bulky weight
Gauge: Working in rounds of stockinette stitch (st st) and with larger dpns,
  5 sts and 7 rnds = 1 inch.
Skill level: Intermediate

total cost

yarn	$3.29
knitting needles	3.00
yarn needle	.50
total	$6.79

here's how
1 For mittens (make two): With smaller dpns and main color, cast on 28 (32, 36)
   sts. Arrange the sts onto 3 dpns; join and place a marker to indicate the
   beginning of rnd. Work around in k 1, p 1 ribbing for 2 (2½, 2½) inches.
2 Change to the larger dpns. Knit every rnd for st st until the piece measures
   2¾ (3½, 3½) inches from beginning.
3 For thumb, slip 6 sts onto holder; cast on 6 sts; k around = 28 (32, 36) sts.
   Work even to 4¾ (6, 6½) inches from beginning.
4 For shaping, Rnd 1: (K 2, k 2 tog) around. Rnd 2: K 21 (24, 27) sts. Rnd 3: (K 1,
   k 2 tog) around. Rnd 4: K 14 (16, 18) sts. Rnd 5: (K 2 tog) around = 7 (8, 9) sts.
5 Cut yarn leaving 8-inch tail. Thread tail into needle and back through
   remaining sts. Pull up to gather; close top opening. Secure.
6 To complete thumb, k 6 sts from holder, pick up and k 6 more sts around
   opening. Arrange the 12 sts onto three dpns; join. Work around in st st until
   thumb measures 1¼ (1½, 1¾) inches from beginning. K 2 tog around. Leaving a
   6-inch tail, cut yarn. Thread tail into yarn needle and back through remaining sts.
7 Using the duplicate stitch chart, *left,* count stitches on mitten top to center
   pattern and embroider backs with white yarn. Weave loose ends on wrong side
   of knitting.

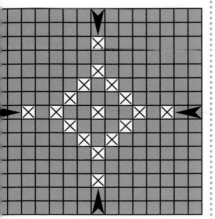

duplicate stitch chart

colorful
(35) candle tin

Decorate your kitchen by intermixing cherries and votive candles in a muffin tin.

what you'll need
Votive candles
Miniature-muffin pan
Artificial cherries
1 yard of ¼-inch-wide ribbon

here's how
1 Place votive candles as desired into the muffin pan. Arrange artificial cherries between the candles. Be careful to space fruit safely away from candlewicks.
2 Tie a bow with ribbon ends. Arrange the ribbon around the pan.

Note: Never leave burning candles unattended.

total cost

candles	$2.89
muffin tin	2.49
artificial cherries	1.00
ribbon	.59
total	$6.97

(36) bejeweled trees

Nest flea market jewelry in glass tree jars for an inviting holiday accent.

what you'll need
Candle, optional
Clear glass tree jar
Flea market jewelry

here's how
1 If using a candle in the jar, center it in the bottom. Stabilize the candle by placing jewelry around it, avoiding the wick area.
2 If using the jar lid, fill the bottom of the jar with jewelry and place a few pieces in the lid so the tree is decorated to the top. Carefully place the lid on the jar.

Note: Never leave burning candles unattended.

total cost

jar	$1.99
jewelry	2.49
total	$4.48

37 copper tree

Hanging from a bag or on a chain around your neck, this copper tree makes a bold contemporary statement.

what you'll need
Needle-nose pliers
Copper wire; hammer
2 metal beads
Ribbon or chain

total cost

copper wire	$ 1.50
beads	.10
ribbon or chain	.25
total	$1.85

here's how

1 Using needle-nose pliers, bend wire back and forth in graduated widths to form a tree shape. Leave a 2-inch straight piece of wire at the top. Twist the end at the bottom into a curl.

2 Place the tree on a hard, flat work surface, such as a metal vise or anvil. Hammer the wire flat except for the 2-inch length at the top.

3 Slip beads on the end of the wire at the top. Bend the end of the wire to form a hanging loop.

4 Tie a ribbon to the top of the wire or slip a chain through the loop to wear as a necklace.

38
simply beautiful ornaments

Make dancing stars in minutes using ordinary ball ornaments and metallic paint pens.

what you'll need
Soft cloth
Matte-finish glass ornaments in desired color
Small-mouth drinking glass
Metallic paint marking pen

here's how
1 Using a soft cloth, gently wipe any dust from the ornaments. If using glass balls, handle them with care as some glass ornaments are fragile and break easily. While working, place each ball in a drinking glass to prevent rolling.
2 Draw a design on the balls using a paint pen. Draw stars, scallops, small dots, zigzags, words, or curlicues. Work on one side at a time. Let dry.
3 Turn the balls over in the glasses and finish the other sides. Let dry.

total cost

ornaments	$3.50
paint marking pen	2.89
total	$6.39

(39) berried candles

Create holiday magic by wrapping candlelight in the colors of the season.

what you'll need
Tall clear glass candleholders; clear glass tumblers
Adhesive for glass
Wired artificial greenery with berries
Wire cutters; 1½-inch-wide sheer ribbon; scissors
Votive candles

here's how
1 Glue a tumbler to the top of each candleholder. Let the adhesive dry.
2 Wrap the tumbler bases with greenery, twisting the wire ends to secure. Cut off any excess greenery.
3 Tie a ribbon bow to one side of greenery. Trim ribbon ends. Insert votive candle.

Note: Never leave burning candles unattended.

total cost

candleholder	$3.99
tumbler	1.00
greenery	1.49
ribbon	.59
votive candle	.50
total	$7.57

④⓪trailing stars

Suspend graduated sizes of stars from beaded wire to make striking tree ornaments.

what you'll need
Electric drill and ¹⁄₁₆-inch bit
Purchased unfinished wood stars in small, medium, and large sizes
Metallic gold crafts wire
Wire cutters; seed beads
Assorted large beads
Thick white crafts glue; paintbrush
Glitter in red or silver

total cost

stars	$ .99
wire	.10
glitter	2.00
beads	.45
total	$3.54

here's how
1 Drill a small hole in the top and bottom of each of the stars.
2 To make the hanging loop, cut a piece of wire 5 inches in length and thread approximately 1 inch through top of large star. Twist to secure next to hole.
3 Thread several seed beads on the other end of the wire. Place the open end of wire between thumb and index finger, pinch, and twist several times into a circle to make a curly loop.
4 Cut a 2-inch length of wire; thread one end through bottom hole of large star. Thread on several seed beads and thread the other end into the top hole of the medium star. Twist and secure. Repeat process to attach medium and small stars. Wire on one or two larger beads to bottom of small star.
5 Thin glue with water; coat stars. While wet, sprinkle with glitter. Let dry.

Vintage linens find their place during the holidays transforming into lovely Christmas stockings. Dainty lace and satin ribbons drape from each cuff's edge.

total cost

tea towel	$4.89
napkin	1.49
lace	1.29
ribbon	.49
total	**$8.16**

what you'll need
Tracing paper; pencil
Scissors
18×28-inch vintage or new tea towel for stocking
Ruler
Vintage or new fabric napkin or tea towel for cuff
Sewing machine
30 inches of lace; sewing needle and thread
36 inches of ⅛- or ¼-inch-wide ribbon

here's how
1 Enlarge and trace the pattern, *below left,* and cut out. Use the pattern to cut two stocking shapes from the tea towel. Cut a 1×5-inch piece of fabric for a hanging loop. Cut two corners from napkin or tea towel, each equal to the width of the stocking top and approximately half the stocking height.
2 Stitch the stocking pieces with the right sides together using ¼-inch seams. Leave the top open. Clip and trim the seam. Turn the stocking to the right side.
3 For the hanging loop, press in ¼ inch along two long edges. Press in half lengthwise and topstitch. Fold the loop in half crosswise and baste the raw edge at the back seam. Seam the cuff in a continuous loop.
4 Stitch lace along the bottom edge of cuff. Weave ribbon through the lace if desired and tie into a bow.
5 Match the side seams with the right side of the cuff to the wrong side of stocking. Stitch around the top edge. Fold the cuff to the right side.

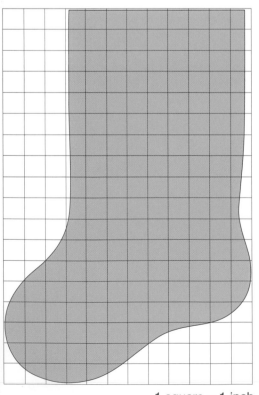

1 square = 1 inch
(enlarge 125%)

⓸2 jingle-jangle trims

A twist on the traditional red and white, jingle bells make these trims sparkle with silver and golden tones.

total cost

jingle bells	$3.59
crafts wire	.25
beaded wire	.50
ribbon	1.00
total	$5.34

what you'll need
Crafts wire; ruler; wire cutters; needle-nose pliers
Assorted sizes of jingle bells in gold and silver
Beaded wire; ½-inch-wide ribbon in gold and silver

here's how
1 Measure crafts wire to the desired length for ornament and cut with wire cutters. Using needle-nose pliers, pinch one end of the wire and twist to create a small loop.
2 Thread different sizes and colors of bells onto the wire until approximately ¼ inch of the wire is left at the end. Use pliers to shape a small loop in the wire end.
3 Bend one end of the ornament so the shape resembles a candy cane. Measure approximately 6 inches of beaded wire and loop it around the top curve of the ornament. Secure it with needle-nose pliers.
4 Tie a ribbon bow around the middle of the cane.

43 friendly fellas

Topped with hats made from socks, these smiling snowmen warm hearts all winter long.

what you'll need
Sock; scissors
Round white glass ornament
Hot-glue gun and glue sticks
Pom-poms in green, red, or silver
Fishing line or thread; yarn needle; yarn
Pink makeup blush; wire cutters
Black permanent marking pen
Orange plastic-coated wire; sharpened
  pencil

total cost

sock	$1.00
ornament	1.00
pom-poms	.50
yarn	.05
wire	.50
total	$3.05

here's how
1 Cut off the cuff portion of the sock, approximately 5 inches from the top. Stretch the cuff piece over the glass ornament, covering the hook. Fold back a ½-inch cuff. Hot-glue the sock in place, allowing enough room for the snowman face. To trim the hat, hot-glue pom-poms on it as desired.
2 For a hanging loop, cut and tie fishing line through the loop on the ornament. Knot the ends to secure.
3 To finish cap, gather 1 to 2 inches from the top with yarn. Pull snug and knot the yarn ends. If desired, fringe the top cap piece.
4 Draw a face on ornament with marking pen. Apply blush for cheeks.
5 For nose, wrap orange wire around pencil tip, allowing the tip to gradually get smaller. Cut with wire cutters. Hot-glue nose in place.

(44) frontdoor frosty

This friendly fellow loves hanging out at your front door to melt your heart with a smile all winter long.

what you'll need

Metal snowman-shape cake pan
Newspapers
White spray primer for metal
Acrylic paints for metal in white, black, and pink
Paintbrush; artificial snow flecks
⅛ yard red and green plaid flannel fabric; scissors; ruler
Thick white crafts glue
1-inch red pom-pom; two 1-inch black buttons; braid
Two ⅝-inch black shank buttons
4-inch-square piece of green felt
Scrap of red felt

here's how

1 Wash and dry the cake pan. In a well-ventilated work area, cover surface with newspapers. Spray-paint the outside of the pan with primer. Let the primer dry. Spray on a second coat of primer. Let dry.
2 Mix some white acrylic paint with artificial snow flecks. Using the photo, *opposite,* as a guide, paint the snowman body with the paint. Let the paint dry. Paint the details on the snowman. Let the paint dry.
3 Cut two strips of fabric, approximately 4 inches long and 3 inches wide. Fold and shape the fabric into a scarf and glue it in place. Glue the pom-pom, buttons, and braid in place.
4 From green felt, cut two holly leaf shapes. Cut three circles from red felt for berries. Glue the felt pieces on the hat. Let dry.

total cost

cake pan	$4.99
paints and primer	2.56
assorted fabric and trims	1.89
total	$9.44

(45) seashell tree topper

A fun and unexpected departure, this shell tree topper glistens with color and texture.

total cost

foam cone	$1.99
shells	1.89
paints	3.99
ribbon	.79
total	**$8.66**

what you'll need
Sharp knife; foam cone, such as Styrofoam, in desired size
Assortment of shells, including a starfish
Newspapers; metallic gold spray paint
Transparent glass paints, in desired colors; paintbrush
Hot-glue gun and glue sticks
1 yard of wide ribbon; scissors; quilting pins

here's how
1 Using a sharp knife, cut the foam cone in half lengthwise. Each topper will use one half of the cone.
2 Wash and dry shells. In a well-ventilated work area, place shells on newspapers. Spray the shells with gold paint. Let dry and spray again if needed. Let dry.
3 Using the photograph, *above,* as a guide, determine shell pattern and placement, planning smaller shells for the top of the cone. Paint the shells with glass paints. Let dry.
4 Starting at the bottom, hot-glue the shells to the rounded side of the foam cone.
5 Cut three strips of ribbon, each approximately 12 inches long. Centering the ribbons in horizontal rows on the back of the foam, pin the ribbons securely across the foam.
6 Use the ribbon ends to secure the topper to the tree.

pinecone place cards

Dinner guests feel ever so welcome with these natural place cards by their plates.

what you'll need
Metallic acrylic paints in blue, purple, gold, copper, green, or other desired colors
Paintbrush
Pinecones; acorns
Medium-weight paper scrap
Ruler
Gold metallic marking pen

total cost

pinecones and acorns	$1.00
paints	2.59
marking pen	1.39
total	$4.98

here's how

1 Paint the pinecones the desired color. Paint the tops and bottoms of the acorns different colors. Let the paint dry.

2 For each place card, tear a 1½×3-inch piece of paper. Wet the edges with water. Paint the edges of the paper, allowing the paint to bleed. Let dry. Write a name in the center of the paper using a gold metallic marking pen.

3 For each place card, set the pinecone in a position on a table to avoid rolling. Insert the paper place card in the top of the pinecone. Arrange the acorns around the pinecone.

47 pretty pasta tree

With as many colors as a rainbow, this ornamental table tree is made from oodles of noodles.

what you'll need
Waxed paper
Assorted pasta in interesting shapes
Thick white crafts glue
Wood skewer
Plastic cone approximately 12 inches tall
Sponge or standard brush for glue
Newspapers; black spray paint
Acrylic gloss paints in desired colors
Paintbrush

here's how
1 Create the treetop star first. Lay shell pasta on waxed paper and arrange in a star shape, gluing generously between shells. Glue a skewer in between two shells for inserting into the cone.
2 To make the tendrils, partially boil long strands of pasta. Boil just long enough so they are flexible. Pat dry. Shape noodles and lay flat until dry. Generously glue onto the star, inserting the ends between shells. Let dry. Glue shells to the back side of star so it looks the same from both sides. Insert end of skewer into top of cone.
3 Use a sponge or regular brush to apply a very thick coat of crafts glue onto surfaces of cone, working on one section at a time. (It is important to cover the entire foam surface with glue to prevent the spray paint from eating into the foam.) Begin covering the cone with pasta. Arrange pasta in rows, using a variety of textures and shapes. Let dry.
4 In a well-ventilated work area, cover work surface with newspapers. Spray entire tree with black spray paint. Let dry. Repeat if necessary to get paint into all the deep crevices. Let the paint dry.
5 Paint rows of pasta different colors, allowing the black crevices to show. If desired, layer some of the paint colors, such as yellow over orange, lime green over blue, or red over purple. Allow the first layer of paint to dry; then paint the second color over the first, letting some of the first color show.

total cost

pasta	$3.65
skewer	.15
plastic cone	1.99
paints	4.20
total	$9.99

⃝48 rose corsage

Any lady feels as
pretty as a
princess wearing
this elegant
corsage.

what you'll need
2 yards of 1½-inch-wide red felt wire-edge ribbon
Yardstick
Scissors
Needle and matching thread
10 inches each of 1½-inch-wide felt wire-edge ribbon in two
  shades of green
4-inch length of 1½-inch-wide wire-edge ribbon for back
Two 4-inch-long sprays of vintage artificial corsage leaves with
  fruit trim

here's how
1 Cut red ribbon into 1-yard lengths for each rose. Pull out the
  wire along one edge of each piece.
2 With wireless edge at the bottom, fold down one end of ribbon
  to extend ½ inch below the bottom edge.
3 For flower center, wind ribbon from end that is folded down
  clockwise several times and hand-stitch to secure.
4 Fold back length of ribbon close to flower center and wind
  several times. Fold back ribbon again and wind again. Use
  running stitches to gather the remaining length of ribbon and
  wind around center. Taper and
  secure ribbon end with hand
  stitches. Make two roses.
5 For leaves, remove wire from
  one edge of a 10-inch length
  of green ribbon. Fold ribbon
  in half crosswise. Make a
  running stitch from the
  folded edge with wire curving
  down to unwired edge and
  curving back up to wired
  edge. Trim away corners of
  bottom edge.
6 Gather leaf and secure
  thread. Open leaf and shape
  along wired edge. Make
  two leaves.
7 Assemble roses and leaves
  and hand-stitch to 4-inch
  ribbon piece. Using the
  photo, *left,* as a guide,
  hand-stitch artificial corsage
  leaves with fruit trim in place.

total cost

ribbons	$3.16
corsage leaves/fruit	1.98
total	$5.14

49 ribbon purse

Just the right size for holding a small surprise, this bag is woven from scraps of holiday ribbons.

what you'll need
Scissors; ruler; ¼ yard of lightweight fusible interfacing; pins
Corrugated cardboard
Approximately 9 yards of ¼- to 1½-inch-wide ribbons
Fusible hem tape; iron; 7×9-inch lining fabric; thread; sewing machine
Needle; snap; button; tassel

total cost

interfacing	$ .60
ribbons	4.41
hem tape	.50
lining fabric	.50
snap and button	.50
tassel	.65
total	$7.16

here's how

1 Cut a 6½×22½-inch piece of interfacing. Pin it fusible side up to the cardboard. Cut enough 22½-inch-long ribbons to cover the interfacing. Pin the ribbons side by side atop the interfacing.

2 Cut several ribbons to a length of 6½ inches. Pin hem tape to the ribbon backs. Begin weaving short ribbons with those pinned to cardboard. Pin ribbon ends as woven. Using an iron, fuse ribbons to interfacing, removing pins as you go. Trim edges.

3 Place the lining onto the woven piece, right sides facing. Stitch together using a ¼-inch seam allowance and leaving one short end open. Trim seams and turn. Measure 4½ inches from stitched short end. Fold the woven piece at this point with right sides facing. Hand-stitch both side seams. Turn right side out.

4 To make the flap point, measure 2½ inches from open end on each side. Fold the corners together and stitch from sides to center of flap. Turn right side out. Sew on a snap where flap point meets bag. Sew a button and tassel to point of flap.

star cornucopias

These lightweight paper ornaments hold a variety of holiday treasures, such as small trims and candies.

what you'll need
Tracing paper
Pencil
Scissors
7-inch squares of decorative papers
Thick white crafts glue
Crafts knife
12 inches of thin metallic gold ribbon

here's how
1 Trace the full-size pattern, *opposite,* onto tracing paper and cut out. Trace around the pattern on the wrong side of the decorative paper. Cut and fold along the pattern lines.
2 Cut five triangle star points out of a contrasting decorative paper. Glue them to the wrong side of the star points. Let dry. Apply glue to the right side of the flap and then tuck it

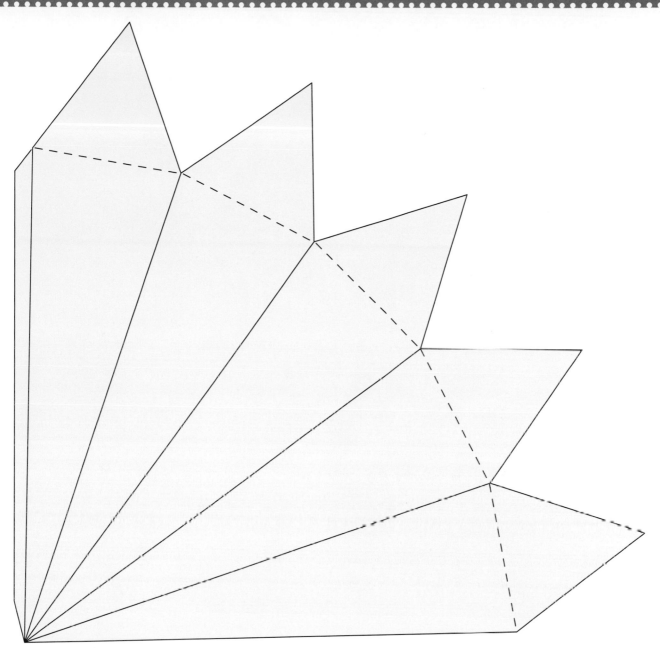

cornucopia pattern

behind the first cornucopia point. Let dry. With a crafts knife, cut slits below two star points on opposite sides of cornucopia.

3 For the handle, knot one end of a 12-inch-long piece of ribbon. Then thread the other end in through one slit and out through the other. Knot the end to hold the handle in place.

total cost

papers	$1.99
ribbon	1.00
total	**$2.99**

51 festive floss trims

Vivid embroidery floss enhances the shapes of purchased wood or plastic ornaments. In an evening make a set for your tree or to give as a much-appreciated gift.

what you'll need
Thick white crafts glue
Paintbrush
Wood or plastic ornament in desired shape or curtain ring with screw eye
Embroidery floss in desired colors
Scissors
1-inch-wide sheer wire-edge ribbon
Large marking pen or dowel

here's how
1 Paint on a thin layer of glue at one end of the ornament. Begin winding the desired color of floss around the glued area. Continue gluing and wrapping floss around ornament, changing colors as you wish. The floss ends should be glued down securely. Let dry.
2 Tie a ribbon bow to the ornament top. Smooth out the ribbon tails. Wrap the tails around a large marking pen or dowel to create curls on the ends.

total cost

ornament	$1.99
floss	2.50
ribbon	1.00
total	$5.49

star napkin rings

Give a rustic theme to a Hanukkah table setting with star napkin rings formed from sticks.

what you'll need
Pliable twigs approximately ⅛ inch in diameter
Twig cutter; sharp knife
34-gauge wire; 18-gauge wire; ruler
Wire cutters
Needle-nose pliers

here's how
1 Beginning at the end of one twig, bend it four times at 2½-inch intervals. Cut it at the fourth bend.
2 Whittle the sides for the first and last sections so they lie flat against each other when they overlap.
3 Using 34-gauge wire and needle-nose pliers, fasten the overlapping twig sections to each other, forming an equilateral triangle.
4 Cut a second twig to the same length and bend at the same 2½-inch intervals. Whittle as in Step 2, *above*. Weave the second twig into the first triangle, centering the points of the second triangle on the sides of the first. Wire the overlapping sides together as before.
5 To make a wire loop for the napkin ring, use a piece of 18-gauge wire about 3½ inches long. Use needle-nose pliers to squeeze one end of the wire around the star where the triangles cross; repeat on the opposite side, shaping the wire into a half circle.

total cost

wire	$ .10
total	$ .10

⑤③ battenberg mantel

Drape a shelf with a lace edge made from a tablecloth embellished with colorful stitches and buttons.

what you'll need
Purchased 36-inch Battenberg lace tablecloth
Assorted machine embroidery threads in rayon and gold metallic
Assorted crafts buttons
Sewing needle and thread

here's how
1 Following the edge of the tablecloth design, stitch rows of embroidery threads, using different colors and stitches.
2 Sew on buttons where appropriate to enhance the Battenberg design on the tablecloth.

total cost

tablecloth	$4.99
threads	2.00
buttons	1.50
total	$8.49

54 heart pins

Create miniature pieces of art to give with love. These colorful resin hearts are simply luminous.

total cost

art board and papers	$4.25
resin and hardener	2.50
gems	.75
glitter paint	.50
wire	.10
beads	.30
pin back	.15
total	$8.55

what you'll need
Black art board
Scissors
Adhesive-back papers, such as foil, metallic, and hologram papers
Decorative-edge scissors
Pencil
Waxed paper
Liquid plastic casting resin and hardener
Crafts stick
Gems
Metallic gold glitter fabric paint
Fine wire; colored beads
Hot-glue gun and glue sticks
Pin backs

here's how
1 To make several pins at one time, start with a piece of black art board in desired size.
2 Cut the papers into small, irregular shapes. Use decorative-edge scissors to cut long strips of paper. Remove backing after cutting.
3 Arrange papers in a random pattern to cover black art board, allowing small black borders to show between the pieces.
4 Draw heart shapes on paper-covered board as many times as possible. Cut out.
5 In a well-ventilated work area, place waxed paper on work surface and arrange heart shapes. Mix the resin and hardener following the manufacturer's instructions. Use a crafts stick to spread a thick coat of resin on each heart. Before it begins to set, press in gems. Let hearts set overnight.
6 Outline hearts and gems with glitter paint. Let dry. String beads onto fine wire. Loop ends of wire around first and last beads and back into strand of beads. Hot-glue onto back of heart. Curl and shape wired beads. Repeat for each heart. Hot-glue one pin back to back of each heart.

55 fancy floral frame

Surprise someone special on Valentine's Day with a pasta-embellished picture frame that's budding with tenderness.

what you'll need
Newspapers; bright pink spray paint
Wide picture frame with white inset
  or mat
Alphabet macaroni, acini di pepe,
  shells, elbow macaroni, and ditalini
Strong adhesive, such as E6000
Acrylic enamel paints in desired colors
Paintbrush

total cost

frame	$2.99
pasta	.75
paints	2.50
total	$6.24

here's how
1 In a well-ventilated work area, cover work surface with newspapers. Spray-paint the frame. Let dry.
2 Glue alphabet macaroni on the inset or mat to spell BE MINE, placing and X and O between phrases. Let dry.
3 To make a petaled flower, glue five shells in a circle. Glue ditalini in the center. Attach shell leaves. Let dry.
4 To make a rose, hook together two pieces of elbow macaroni. Add three thin elbows to complete the circle. Make an elbow stem and shell leaves. Glue in place. Let dry.
5 Glue pieces of acini di pepe between the flowers. Let dry.
6 Using the photo, *above,* as a guide, paint the pasta pieces. Let dry.

Welcome spring with crafts projects that brighten the spirit. Paint a May basket that was once a drinking cup. Decoupage a flea market serving tray with dainty pansies. Stitch pretty stationery to keep in touch with special friends. All this and more awaits in this cheery chapter.

spring

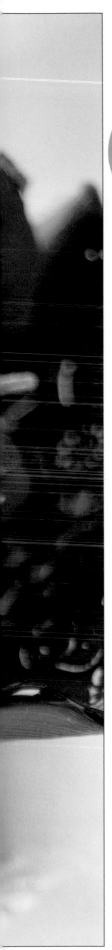

(56) strawberry sachets

Speckled with clear seed beads, these sweetly scented strawberries are always in season.

what you'll need
White pencil
Cereal bowl
¼ yard crinkle red cotton lamé
Scissors
Needle
Thread in red and green
Sheet of felt
Strawberry-scented oil
Fiberfill
Thin needle to fit through beads
Clear seed beads
⅛ yard green cotton lamé
22-gauge floral wire; ruler

total cost

red lamé	$1.00
felt	.25
scented oil	1.99
fiberfill	.25
seed beads	.25
green lamé	.50
floral wire	.25
total	$4.49

here's how
1 Use a white pencil to trace around the edge of a cereal bowl on the red fabric. Remove the bowl and cut out the traced circle.
2 Use a needle threaded with red thread to stitch a running stitch around the edge of the fabric circle. Pull both the beginning and end of the thread to gather the fabric circle into a berry shape.
3 Cut a 1-inch-thick strip across the width of the felt. Dab a drop of scented oil onto one end of the felt strip. Starting with the oiled end, roll up the felt strip and then place it in the center of the gathered fabric. Stuff pinches of fiberfill around the felt to widen the top of the strawberry. When the shape is formed as desired, pull both ends of the thread tightly over the stuffing and knot them together.
4 Thread a thin needle with red thread to begin stitching the white beads on the outside of the strawberry. Avoid piercing the rolled felt in the center of the strawberry with the needle to prevent the scented oil from spreading and leaking onto the red fabric.
5 Draw a circle on green lamé to cover top of a strawberry; trim the edge in a zigzag fashion. Snip a small slit in the center of the leaf. Cut a 3-inch length of floral wire and then fold the wire in half. Coil the two wire ends into small circles. Thread the folded end of the floral wire stem through the slit in the leaf. Position the leaf on top of the beaded strawberry with the wire ends down. Stitch the leaf and stem in place with a needle and green thread.

57 silk scarf pillow

Choose a scarf to match your decor instead of your outfit and sew a beautiful quilted pillow.

total cost

scarf	$2.00
cotton fabric	.75
batting	1.30
pillow form	2.50
fringe	2.99
beads	.25
total	$9.79

what you'll need

Silk scarf at least 15 inches square
½ yard of coordinating cotton fabric for lining and back
16-inch square of quilt batting
Metallic gold sewing machine thread
Sewing machine; ruler or measuring tape; scissors
2 yards of beaded sew-in fringe
Pillow form; 5mm accent beads; needle

here's how

1 Line the scarf with cotton fabric and batting. Machine-quilt around scarf design using metallic gold thread.
2 Trim quilted scarf to measure 15 inches square.
3 Using ½-inch seam allowances, sew the beaded fringe around the outside edge. Cut backing fabric the same as the front.
4 Stitch the back to the front, right sides facing, leaving an opening for turning. Trim the corners. Turn to the right side. Insert the pillow form. Stitch opening closed.
5 Sew on accent beads to detail the pillow.

58 teacup napkin

Grace a cloth napkin with vintage flair by transferring on blue work in a classic teacup design.

what you'll need
100-percent cotton napkin with
  eyelet-hemmed edge; iron
Iron-on blue-work teacup design
  (available in fabric stores)
Scissors
Press cloth; tapestry needle
3 yards of 4mm blue silk ribbon

total cost

napkin	$1.00
blue-work design	1.50
silk ribbon	3.00
total	$5.50

here's how
1 Prewash the napkin without using bleach. Let the napkin dry.
  Press the napkin. Follow the manufacturer's instructions to
  transfer the teacup design to one corner of the napkin.
2 Cut away the excess of the textured velour past the edge of the
  design. To iron on the design, heat a dry iron to the wool setting.
3 Thread the ribbon in a tapestry needle. Weave the ribbon
  through the eyelet hem. Knot ends together and trim away the
  excess ribbon.

59 nap-time notice

Make an endearing sign to let everyone know when baby's asleep.

what you'll need
Tracing paper; pencil
Scissors
Heavy cardboard
Fiberfill sheet
Fabric glue
¼ yard of light blue silk shantung
Sewing machine; thread
Dressmaker's carbon
2–3 yards of small pearls on a string
Hot-glue gun and glue sticks
¾ yard of thick decorative cord
Small rhinestones

here's how
1 Enlarge and trace the heart pattern, *above right.* Cut out the shape and trace twice onto cardboard and once onto fiberfill. Cut out the heart shapes. Spot-glue the fiberfill heart to the top of one of the cardboard hearts using fabric glue.
2 Trace the heart pattern twice onto fabric. Machine-stitch on the lines. Cut out both fabric hearts ½ inch from the stitching.
3 Use the dressmaker's carbon to transfer the letters onto one of the hearts.
4 Lay the heart with words over the top of the cardboard heart with fiberfill. Line up stitching to edges of cardboard. Pull fabric over edge of cardboard; hot-glue to back, clipping as needed.
5 Cover the second cardboard heart with the second fabric heart in the same manner for the backing. Set aside.
6 Working one letter at a time, hot-glue the string of pearls over the transferred letters, cutting the length of pearls as needed.
7 For the hanger, cut a 10-inch length of pearls and hot-glue the ends to the back side of the heart. Hot-glue the backing to the heart.
8 Begin at the dip of the heart and hot-glue cord around the outside edge of the heart. Finish with a knot to cover the raw edge of the cord.
9 Randomly glue the small rhinestones across the front of the heart.

1 square = 1 inch   (enlarge 200%)

total cost

fiberfill	$ .25
silk shantung	2.00
pearls on string	3.29
cord	.75
rhinestones	.45
total	$6.74

pretty pansy tray

Serve guests in style with this vintage-looking serving tray lined in pansy motifs.

total cost

photocopies	$3.00
tray	5.99
total	$8.99

what you'll need
Color photocopies of vintage or new floral-motif cards
Scissors
Distressed-look serving tray
Thick white crafts glue
Paintbrush
Dried, pressed pansies and ferns

here's how
1 Trim photocopies as desired. Arrange trimmed pieces on the top of a serving tray.
2 Keeping the desired arrangement, glue the paper pieces in place. Let dry.
3 Arrange and glue on pressed pansies and ferns where desired. Let dry. Thin glue with water; coat decoupaged areas of tray. Let the glue dry.

61 dainty watering cans

Tiny enough to hold in the palm of your hand, this mini arrangement blooms with cheer.

what you'll need
Disposable plate
Acrylic enamel paints in white and other desired color
Sea sponge
Miniature watering can
Color photocopies of fresh flowers
Scissors
Thick white crafts glue
Paintbrush
Metallic silver or gold marking pen
Small plastic cup

total cost

paints	$2.89
sponge	.39
watering can	1.49
photocopies	1.00
marking pen	1.89
total	$7.66

here's how
1 Place small amounts of paints on a disposable plate. Moisten the sponge and wring out excess water.
2 Dab sponge lightly in each paint color; dab onto watering can. Continue applying color in this manner until the desired look is achieved. Let dry.
3 Cut out photocopies of flowers. Arrange cutouts as desired on watering can. Glue cutouts in place. Let dry. Thin glue with water; coat the front of the cutouts. Let dry.
4 Accent the edges of the watering can with tiny stripes drawn with a silver or gold marking pen. Trace the flower outline with pen. Let dry.
5 Before placing flowers in the can, place a small plastic cup inside can. Fill with tiny flowers and water.

62

dainty posy box

Fill this clay-embellished box to the brim with aromatic potpourri for an irresistible display.

what you'll need
White air-dry clay, such as Crayola Model Magic
Rolling pin
Small heart-shape cookie cutter
Butter knife
Thick white crafts glue
3½-inch high round cardboard box with lid approximately 6 inches in diameter
Acrylic paints in desired colors
Fine-point and small, flat paintbrushes
White gel stain; damp, soft cloth

total cost

clay	$1.20
box	1.99
paints and stain	4.19
total	$7.38

here's how
1 Roll out clay to a thickness of approximately ³⁄₁₆ inch. Cut out four small hearts with cookie cutter. Set aside to dry.
2 Shape leaves by forming a marble-size ball out of clay. Flatten it into an oval shape and press a crease into the center with the blade of a knife. Let dry.
3 Form seven or eight small balls to place in the center of the flower. To make the blue flowers around the edge, form five balls of clay for each flower. Shape tiny leaves out of clay. Let dry.
4 Glue clay shapes onto the lid and sides of the box.
5 Coil a piece of clay into a ⅛-inch-thick rope to trim the edge of lid. Place a thin line of glue around the edge and adhere the rope of clay around the edge, meeting at each flower. Let the clay dry on the box.
6 Paint the entire box, inside and out, using white. Let the paint dry. Paint the box pale yellow. Slightly overlap the paint onto the flowers and rope. Let the paint dry. Paint the large flowers red, the leaves and rope green, the small flowers blue, and the flower centers bright yellow. Let the paint dry.
7 Coat the entire outside of the box and the lid using a generous amount of white gel stain. Brush the gel stain into all of the crevices of the clay design.
8 Let the gel just begin to dry and gently wipe off with the damp, soft cloth. Wipe just enough to take the top surface off, leaving the white stain in the crevices. Let the stain dry.

63 pretty pencil holder

Artful motifs cut from decorative papers beautify this set of pencils and holder.

total cost

toothbrush holder	$4.99
papers	1.00
pencils	1.00
glass paint	1.50
total	**$8.49**

what you'll need
Toothbrush holder
Scissors
Scraps of decorative scrapbook or origami papers
Thick white crafts glue
Pencils
Glass paint; paintbrush

here's how
1 Wash and dry toothbrush holder.
2 Using scissors, cut out flowers or other motifs from decorative paper and glue onto the holder.
3 Cut paper to cover each pencil, allowing a slight overlap. Glue the paper around each pencil.
4 Dip the handle of a paintbrush into paint and dot the center of each flower. Place dots in groups of three between the flowers. Let the paint dry.

64 tiny tote

Dress up a tiny canvas tote with clusters of floral and leaf beads.

what you'll need
Thread; scissors; ruler
Beading needle
Mini canvas tote bag
Beads in flower and leaf shapes
Assorted seed and other small beads

total cost

tote bag	$1.99
beads	3.49
total	$5.48

here's how

1 Cut an 18-inch length of thread. Thread the needle and knot one end of the thread.

2 From the inside of the bag, push the needle through one side, centered approximately 1½ inches from the top. Thread on a flower bead and a seed bead. Push the needle back through the flower bead and the bag. Continue attaching bead flowers until you like the look. Sew on single seed beads and leaf beads as desired. Knot the thread on the inside of the bag.

3 Sew bead trims to the tote bag handle in the same manner.

embroidered stationery

A few simple stitches of silk ribbon create charming notes.

what you'll need
Tracing paper; pencil
Card stock note card and matching envelope
Darning needle
4mm or 7mm silk ribbon in desired colors
Fine tapestry needle; glue, optional

here's how
1 Trace design, *opposite,* onto tracing paper. Place the tracing on note card on a protected work surface.
2 Use a darning needle to pierce the design into the paper and note card. Using the pattern holes, stitch diagrams, and the photo, *below* and *opposite,* as guides, stitch the design with silk ribbon, knotting on the back.
3 Trim the envelope and note card with running stitches or flat pieces of ribbon glued in place.

total cost

note card and envelope	$1.00
ribbon	2.00
total	**$3.00**

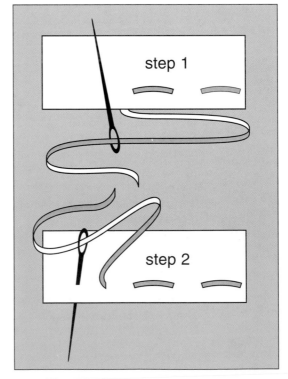

step 1

step 2

running stitch

straight stitch

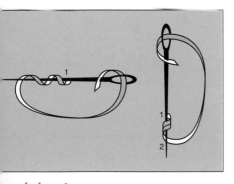
ench knot

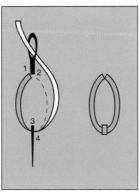
lazy daisy stitch

placement
diagrams

(66) two-tone purse

Contrasting fabrics lend pizzazz to this quilted shoulder bag for springtime.

what you'll need
Paper; scissors; ruler
½ yard of fabric
Thread; sewing machine
14×24-inch piece of contrasting fabric
½ yard quilt batting; ½ yard lining fabric
3 sizes of vintage buttons; needle
10-inch-long piece of ¼-inch wood dowel
3×13-inch piece of mat board, optional

here's how
1 Cut pattern shapes from paper according to diagrams, *below.* Cut fabric pieces as indicated on patterns, adding ½-inch seam allowances and using contrasting fabric as desired. Stitch all pieces with right sides facing unless otherwise indicated.
2 Line purse pieces with quilt batting and machine-quilt as desired. Stitch the front to the back along the bottom edge. Stitch the side pieces along the sides and bottom edge. Repeat for lining.
3 Stitch handle pieces along long edges. Turn to the right side. Stitch a 14-inch-long dart at the top center of the handle. Stitch each end of the handle to the top of the side pieces. Stitch lining to purse along the flap and at the side pieces, leaving the front edge open for turning. Turn to right side. Topstitch opening closed.
4 Fold back flap to make top edge boxing, taking a ¾-inch tuck from side box to side box to create casing for wood dowel. Stitch a ½-inch tuck 1½ inches from dowel casing forming top edge boxing.
5 Attach three stacked buttons for trim to front flap. Insert a wood dowel in casing. If desired, place mat board in the bottom.

total cost

fabrics and batting	$2.50
lining	1.00
dowel	.10
buttons	1.00
total	**$4.60**

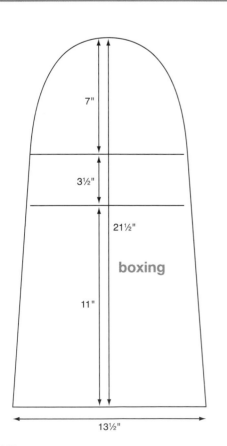

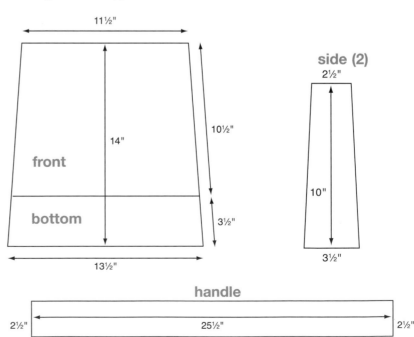

(67) rainbow vase

Choose braid in spring-fresh colors to transform a pitcher into a vase.

total cost

pitcher	$2.49
cord	1.80
ribbon	1.29
total	$5.58

what you'll need
Small glass pitcher
Thick white crafts glue; paintbrush
1 yard variegated braided cord
Scissors
18-inch-long piece of 1½-inch-wide variegated sheer ribbon

here's how
1 Wash and dry the pitcher, removing stopper if necessary.
2 Beginning just below the spout, paint glue on the center portion of the pitcher. Wrap the cording around the pitcher over the glue. Trim the excess cord. Apply more glue to the ends if needed to secure. Let the glue dry.
3 Tie ribbon around the handle. To cut notches into the ribbon ends, fold each of the ends in half lengthwise; cut diagonally.

(68) baby buckets

These endearing pails are just the right size to keep things organized for little darlings.

what you'll need
Off-white acrylic paint; paintbrush
Peat pot (available at
   garden centers)
Baby-motif sticker
Decoupage medium, such as
   Mod Podge; small nail
12 inches of 20-gauge silver wire
Wire cutters
Pencil

total cost

paint	$ .99
peat pot	.14
sticker	1.40
decoupage medium	1.50
wire	3.49
total	$7.52

here's how
1 Brush two coats of paint on the inside and the outside of the pot. Let the paint dry. Apply a third coat to fill any remaining dark spots. Let the paint dry.
2 Apply a sticker to the center front of the bucket. Brush several coats of clear decoupage medium over the sticker. Let dry.
3 Use a small nail to poke a hole on opposite sides of the bucket ½ inch down from the rim. Cut a 12-inch length of the wire for the handle. Wind the center of the wire around a pencil six times. Bend the straight sides of the wire down and thread them through the prepoked holes from the outside. Fold ½ inch of each wire end back up against the handle.

(69) oh-so-sweet may baskets

Metal cans make wonderfully festive containers when painted, embellished with wire handles, and filled with irresistible treats.

what you'll need
Newspapers
Clean fruit or tuna can without lid or sharp edges
Spray paint in desired color
Drill and ¼-inch bit
Paint marker; tube-style paint pens
18-inch lengths of colored wire
⅛-inch dowel or pencil

here's how
1. In a well-ventilated work area, cover work surface with newspapers. Spray-paint the can the desired color. Let dry.
2. Drill a hole on each side of the can just below the rim.
3. Write a name in the center of the can using a paint marker. Draw flowers or other desired designs around the can using paint pens. Let dry.
4. Choose six colored wires to make the handle. With the ends even, group the wires in twos. Beginning 5 inches from one end, braid the handle, leaving 5 inches at the opposite end. Slip the braided wire through the holes in the can. Wrap the unbraided wires around the braided handle once to secure. Wrap the wire ends around a dowel or pencil to curl.

total cost

spray paint	$1.79
paint marker and pens	4.25
wire	1.50
total	$7.54

daisy
may baskets

(70)

Just the right size for a handful of treats, these candy cups are a sweet surprise for those you love.

what you'll need
Newspapers
Acrylic paints in desired colors
Paintbrush
Cone-shape paper cup
Paper punch
Eyelet tool and eyelets
Wood petal shapes
½-inch wood apple shape
¾-inch wood wheel
½-inch wood beads
Hot-glue gun and glue sticks
Pipe cleaners in desired colors
Scissors; pencil

total cost

paints	$1.95
cup	.10
eyelets	.10
wood shapes	2.09
pipe cleaners	.20
total	$4.44

here's how

1 Cover work surface with newspapers. Paint cup desired background color. Let dry. Use a contrasting color to paint a dotted line around the rim. Let dry.

2 Use a paper punch to make a hole ½ inch from rim. Make a second hole opposite the first. From outside of cup, insert an eyelet in each hole. Secure using an eyelet tool.

3 Paint six petal shapes. Paint the apple a contrasting color for flower center. Paint the wheel the same color as flower center and a wood bead the color of petals. Let dry. Hot-glue petals and flower center to the front of the cup. Let dry.

4 Thread an unpainted wood bead onto a pipe cleaner that matches the flower center. Twist the pipe cleaner to secure the bead at one end. Snip off the end of the cup. From the inside push the end of the pipe cleaner through the bottom of the cup. The bead holds it in place.

5 Thread the painted wheel and bead onto the pipe cleaner. Twist remaining stem around a pencil to curl.

6 For a handle, twist two contrasting pipe cleaners together. Insert through the eyelets from outside. Fold ends upward to secure.

(71) elegant eggs

Sparkling heart-shape gems and tiny polka dots team up as a striking duo on this bright yellow egg.

what you'll need for heart egg
Egg
Large needle
Toothpick
Bowl
Acrylic paints in yellow and black
Paintbrush
12–15 red heart-shape gems
Thick white crafts glue

here's how
1 Pierce tiny holes on each end of the egg with the needle. Pierce the egg yolk with a toothpick. Blow the egg white and yolk into a bowl. Rinse and dry the egg.
2 Paint the egg yellow. Let the paint dry.
3 Glue the heart gems randomly on the egg. Let the glue dry.
4 Dip the paintbrush handle into black paint and dot on the egg. Continue placing dots between the hearts as desired. Let the paint dry.

what you'll need for flower egg
Egg; large needle
Toothpick; bowl
Lavender acrylic paint
Paintbrush
18 inches of ⅛-inch-diameter light green decorative cord
Thick white crafts glue
Flower-shape cookie sprinkles

Dot an egg with itty-bitty flowers planted between stripes of satin cord.

here's how
1 Pierce tiny holes on each end of the egg with the needle. Pierce the egg yolk with a toothpick. Blow the egg white and yolk into a bowl. Rinse and dry the egg.
2 Paint the egg lavender. Let the paint dry.
3 Coil and glue cord around the egg. Glue flower-shape sprinkles between the rows of cord. Let the glue dry.

total cost

egg	$ .15
paints	.50
gems	.99
total for heart egg	$1.64
egg	$ .15
paint	.50
cord	.50
sprinkles	.10
total for flower egg	$1.25

(72) floral note cards

Preserve a touch of spring beauty and share it on cheery note cards.

what you'll need
Flowers for pressing, such as Queen Anne's lace and blue delphinium
Heavy book
White spray paint and newspapers, optional
Colored paper scraps
Scissors; glue stick
Paintbrush
1 yard of ½- to 1-inch-wide sheer ribbon
Thick white crafts glue

here's how
1 Press flowers in a heavy book overnight or longer until they are well-pressed and fairly dry. If using Queen Anne's lace and it turns yellower than desired, spray with a light coat of white spray paint in a newspaper-protected, well-ventilated work area. Let it dry.
2 Using the photo, *opposite,* for inspiration, cut one or more colors of paper into the desired size and fold to make a card. Cut squares of different paper colors and arrange on the front if desired. Glue in place using a glue stick.
3 Paint a small amount of water-thinned crafts glue onto the card where the flowers will be placed. Gently lay flower into wet glue. Let it dry. Brush on a second coat of thinned glue over the entire flower and card front. Let the glue dry.
4 Embellish the card with a coordinating ribbon bow. Glue in place with crafts glue.

total cost

papers	$ .75
ribbon	1.00
total	$1.75

(73) scented bath salts

Pamper yourself with beautifully bottled, floral-scented bath salts.

what you'll need
Large bowl
2 cups Epsom salts; 1 cup baking soda
4 drops lavender-scented oil
2×4-inch scrap of white cotton fabric
Food coloring; cookie sheet
Apothecary jar (available in thrift shops)
Vintage baby spoon; 1 yard of ribbon

here's how
1 In a large bowl mix 2 cups Epsom salts and 1 cup baking soda. Dab a few drops of scented oil onto cotton fabric and stir through mixture. Repeat with drops of food coloring. Continue mixing scented oil and food coloring until desired scent and color are achieved. If desired, make two colors of salts to layer in jar.
2 Spread mixture onto a cookie sheet for several hours, stirring several times. Wash and dry the jar. Spoon into jar.
3 Tie baby spoon onto jar with ribbon.
4 To use, dissolve several teaspoons of salts in bathwater.

total cost

salts	$1.25
baking soda	.59
lavender oil	.30
jar	2.00
spoon	1.50
ribbon	.90
total	$6.54

dogwood delights

Dine in style
with this
in-bloom table
setting.

total cost

place mat	$1.89
flowers	1.44
plate and mug	2.99
glass paints	3.28
total	$9.60

what you'll need for place mat
Fabric glue
Stem of small silk dogwoods with leaves
Fabric place mat; scissors

here's how
1 Cut flowers and leaves from stem.
2 Arrange and glue flowers across the top of the place mat using dogwood flower as the focal point. Glue some of the leaves from the flowers in and around the dogwoods.

what you'll need for plate and mug
White ceramic plate and mug; grease pencil
Glass paints, such as Liquitex Glossies, in yellow, white, red, and green
Disposable plate; paintbrushes
Cotton swab

here's how
1 Wash and dry the plate and mug. Avoid touching the areas to be painted.
2 Referring to the photo, *below,* draw dogwood and leaf shapes on the plate and mug using a grease pencil.
3 On the disposable plate, mix a small amount of yellow paint with white to make a light cream color for the flowers. Paint the flower petals. Add a touch of red to cream color and paint outside edges of petals. Highlight the centers of the petals with pure white.
4 Mix green and red together to form a dark green. Use this color to add stamens and pistils to centers of flowers.
5 Mix some of dark green with the cream color and use to paint veins on petals.
6 For leaves, paint one side of the leaf with the dark green. Add a little yellow to the dark green and paint the remaining side of the leaf. Use the same greens to paint stems.
7 Use a cotton swab to carefully remove any visible grease pencil.
8 Set paint according to directions on paint jar.

(75) elegant flowerpot

Choose a pretty pair of satin cords to wrap a terra-cotta flowerpot with color.

what you'll need

4-inch terra-cotta flowerpot
Thick white crafts glue; paintbrush
Approximately 3 yards of
¼-inch-wide light green satin cord
Approximately 6 yards of
¼-inch-wide rose-color satin cord
2-inch rose-color tassel

total cost

flowerpot	$1.29
cords	1.80
tassel	1.29
total	$4.38

here's how

1 Brush glue on the pot. Starting with the green cord, wrap the rim of the pot.
2 Use rose-color cord to wrap the bottom of the pot, starting just below the green and tucking the end of the tassel under the first couple of wraps of the cord. Apply more glue to the ends if needed to secure. Let the glue dry.

everyday towels

Liven up linens with braided cord, lace, ribbon, or any trim that matches your decor.

what you'll need
Purchased day-of-the-week tea towel
1 yard of trim or ribbon; sewing machine; thread

here's how
1 Machine-stitch ribbon or trim along the top and bottom edges of the towel design to create a border, turning under the raw edges.

total cost

towel	$2.00
trim	.75
total	**$2.75**

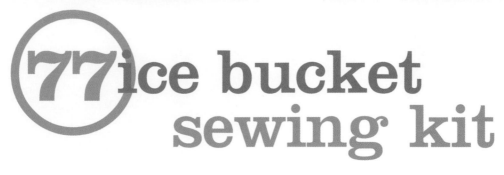

77 ice bucket sewing kit

Keep your sewing tools handy with this clever see-through kit.

what you'll need
Plastic ice bucket approximately 7 inches across the top and 7½ inches high; 2 yards of ⅝-inch-wide satin ribbon
Large tomato pincushion and strawberry emery
Measuring tape; 7×14-inch bias strip of calico
Scissors; needle; thread; green embroidery floss
5-inch square of green calico
Fusible transweb paper; iron
3-inch square scrap of calico to contrast with green
3-inch square of coordinating calico; fabric glue
8×14-inch piece of felt; sewing machine; pinking shears; button

here's how
1 To cover ice bucket handle, tie the center of the 2-yard ribbon to one end of the handle. Bring the ribbon ends to the top side and twist, bringing ribbon ends to the back side in a cross. Repeat to cover the handle, securing the ribbon ends at the opposite end of the handle.
2 To cover the pincushion, measure from the center top to the center bottom and add ¼ inch for seam at bottom. Measure around pincushion at widest part. Add ¼-inch seam at ends and cut bias strip of fabric this measurement.
3 Seam short ends, right sides facing. Stitch gathering threads at bottom edge. Gather bottom. Secure threads and turn to right side. Cover pincushion. Hand-gather top edge and secure threads. Wrap the pincushion with embroidery floss to make tomato seams; knot on bottom.
4 Trace top patterns, *opposite,* on transweb paper and cut out. Cut one each from green calico. Cut off strawberry emery from the pincushion stem, leaving string attached to pincushion. Pierce a hole in the center of the green calico for the top and thread string through the hole; fuse green calico to pincushion top. Cut a quarter circle from contrasting calico and seam the straight edges to cover emery. Turn to right side. Cover emery by gathering around top edge. Pierce hole in green calico for strawberry top. Pull string through hole and reattach to emery. Fuse or glue green calico in place.
5 For scissors case, measure scissors length and width. Cut a rectangle of felt that measurement for case front. Cut case back that measurement plus 3 inches longer for flap. Round the corners at the bottom and for the flap.
6 To make the flower design for the flap, trace the pattern, *opposite,* on transweb paper and cut out. Trace on scrap of calico. Fuse flower to flap. Trim the edge with machine stitches. Cut and stitch a buttonhole in the center of the flower.
7 With wrong sides facing, stitch the case front to the back along the sides and bottom edge using a ¼-inch seam. Trim the edge just beyond the stitching using pinking shears.
8 Sew on a button for closure.

total cost

ice bucket	$4.99
ribbon and button	1.00
pincushion	2.00
embroidery floss	.10
felt and transweb paper	.70
calico	.25
total	$9.04

pincushion top

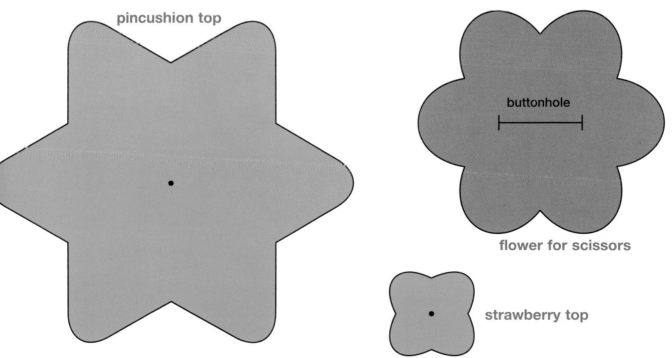

buttonhole

flower for scissors

strawberry top

get ready to be inspired with warm-weather projects for indoors and out. Whether you want to make something colorful to bring sunshine to the table or something playful to invigorate your yard, find the perfect summer project among these blue-ribbon winners.

summer

'78 veggie board

Pick your favorite photo to make artwork out of a clear glass cutting board.

total cost

paper	$1.00
cork	1.10
cutting board	3.69
total	**$5.79**

what you'll need
Newspapers
8½×6½-inch piece of decorative paper
Spray adhesive
9×7-inch sheet of cork
8×6-inch photo
12×9-inch glass cutting board
Strong adhesive, such as E6000

here's how
1 In a well-ventilated work area, cover surface with newspapers. Spray the back of the decorative paper with adhesive. Center the paper on one side of the cork.
2 Spray adhesive on the back of the photo and apply to the center of the decorative paper.
3 Apply glue to the top edges of the cork border and glue to the back of the cutting board. Let the glue dry.

(79) rolled-paper holder

Created in black and white with red accents, this clever kitchen utensil holder is formed from rolled-up magazine pages.

what you'll need
Magazine pages in black and white
¼-inch wood dowel
Glue stick; metal or cardboard can, such as
  a potato stick can
Wooden balls to fit the top of the rolled
  paper tubes, approximately ⅜ inch
Acrylic paints in red and black; paintbrush
Scissors; thick white crafts glue
Black and white twisted plastic-coated wire

total cost

wood balls	$1.49
paints	1.78
wire	.60
total	**$3.87**

here's how
1 Beginning at one corner of the magazine page, roll page diagonally
  around the dowel and glue the corner in place with glue stick. Remove
  dowel. Make enough tubes to go around the can.
2 Paint three wood balls red and the remainder black. You will need one
  ball for each paper tube. Let dry.
3 Cut the tubes to the same height as the container. Using crafts glue,
  adhere the tubes around the side of the can. Glue a ball to the top of
  each tube, placing the red balls randomly in the arrangement.
4 Wrap two bands of wire around the can and knot the ends together.

Create an oversize
butterfly to flutter
among your flowers.

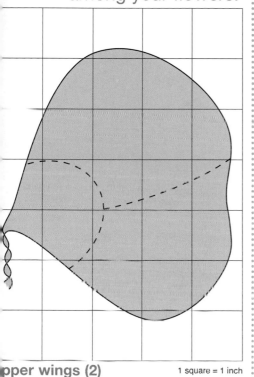

pper wings (2)
nlarge 200%)

1 square = 1 inch

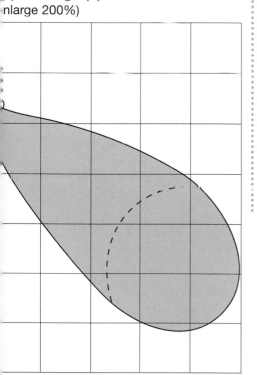

wer wings (2)
nlarge 200%)

1 square = 1 inch

what you'll need

Tracing paper; pencil
Four 18-inch pieces of 18-gauge
cloth-covered florist's wire
½ yard of fabric window screen
Scissors; fabric glue; wire cutters
Metallic gold spray paint
2 yards of metallic gold trim
Sponge; acrylic paints in
copper and turquoise
Metallic gold glitter tube paint
4-inch-long ½-inch-diameter
wood peg or dowel; green florist's tape
6-inch-long piece of thin wire; paintbrush
Acrylic gems; 18-inch piece of 16-gauge florist wire

total cost

wires	$1.50
screen	2.89
paints	2.99
trim	1.29
gems	.99
wood peg	.25
total	$9.91

here's how

1 Enlarge and trace patterns, *left.* Using one cloth-covered wire per wing,
   create four wings following the pattern shapes. Twist ends together.
2 Cut pieces of window screen slightly larger than the wire wings. Apply
   glue to the wire wings and lay over the screen, pressing the edges of
   wire to the screen. Let dry. Trim away excess wire. In a well-ventilated
   area with newspaper covered work surface, spray both sides of the
   wings gold. Let dry.
3 Glue gold trim around the top edge of each wing.
4 Sponge copper paint across each wing. Outline the inside veins with
   gold glitter paint. Let dry.
5 Lay twisted ends of lower wings along the side of the wood peg or
   dowel as shown in Step 1, *below.* Use florist's tape to secure the wings
   to the wood peg.
6 Tape the twisted ends of the upper wings together. Lay the twisted end
   on top of the body above the bottom wings and tape with florist's tape
   as shown in Step 2. Bend thin wire in half and secure to the top end of
   the body while taping on the wings.
7 Paint the body turquoise, painting over the tape. Let dry.
8 Glue gems on wings. Let dry.
9 Make a hook at one end of the 16-gauge wire, large enough to fit over
   the center of the body. Fit the wire over the body, below the upper
   wings. Glue three gems down the center of the body. Use the wire to
   insert the butterfly into the ground or in a potted plant.

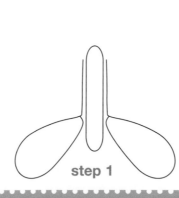

step 1

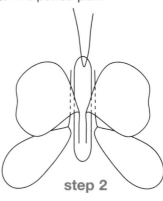

step 2

(81) garden gift tags

Accompany a gift from your garden's bounty with a cheery wood tag.

total cost

veneer	$ .50
permanent marking pens	1.80
raffia	.59
total	$2.89

what you'll need
Scraps of wood veneer; scissors; ruler
Scallop-edge scissors
Paper punch
Paintbrush
Permanent fine-tip marking pens in black, green, and red
12-inch piece of raffia

here's how
1 Cut the veneer into a 5×2½-inch piece. Trim one end with scallop-edge scissors. Punch a hole in the opposite end.
2 Use black marking pen to write message in center of tag. Draw green vines and leaves. Use red for berry-like circles.
3 Thread raffia through the punched hole. Tie to the gift.

82 garden gloves

Pulling weeds is more fun when wearing colorfully painted garden gloves.

what you'll need
Opaque marking pens in desired colors
Vinyl or rubberized gloves
Acrylic paints in desired colors
Paintbrushes

total cost

marking pens	$2.50
gloves	3.49
paints	3.29
total	$9.28

here's how

1 Use opaque marking pens to write gardening words, such as DIG, PLANT, WEED, FEED, WATER, GROW, and HARVEST, randomly across the front of the gloves.

2 Use acrylic paints to paint bulb shapes on two fingers of the gloves. Paint bulbs with white and shade with light brown. Use green paint to paint the beginning of the stem and white for roots. Paint an orange butterfly and outline in black. Let dry.

(83) party snack set

Whether following the design in the glass or making your own pattern, painted cups and plates turn any gathering into a festive gala.

what you'll need
Glass snack tray and coordinating cup (available at antiques stores and thrift shops)
Glass paints, such as Liquitex Glossies, in desired colors
Paintbrushes, including flat and liner
Pencil with round-tip eraser

here's how
1 Wash the glass snack set. Rinse well and let dry. Avoid touching areas you intend to paint.
2 Using the photo, *opposite,* for inspiration, decide how you want to paint the glassware. Paint only the bottom of the tray. On the cup, avoid the rim area and paint on the outside only. Avoid painting areas that will come in contact with food.
3 Paint stripes or dots on the tray before painting background color. To make stripes, use a flat brush for wider stripes and a liner brush for narrow stripes. To make dots, dip the handle of a paintbrush or a pencil eraser into paint and carefully dot onto the surface. Avoid using too much paint or it will run or bubble. To outline areas, use a thin liner brush. Let the paint dry before applying the background color or pattern.
4 To enhance designs raised or embossed in the glass, paint in the patterns. Let dry. Paint the background color.
5 If instructed by the paint manufacturer, bake the painted glassware in the oven. Let it cool.

total cost

glass snack set	$1.99
paints	3.89
total	$5.88

seashell
reflection

(84)

Border your mirror or create a bottle stopper with favorite shells to bring a beach mood to the bath.

what you'll need
Mirror with frame
Seashells
Hot-glue gun and glue sticks
Clear glass bottle or vessel

here's how
1 *For the mirror,* place the shells on the mirror frame, rearranging the shells until the desired look is achieved. Use the photo, *opposite,* for inspiration.
2 Hot-glue the shells in place. Let cool.
3 *For the bottle,* remove the lid or stopper if necessary. Wash and dry the bottle. Place a shell in the top for a stopper.
4 *For the vessel,* wash and dry the container. Fill the vessel to the top with shells.

total cost

mirror	$5.99
shells	2.50
vessel	1.00
total	$9.49

85 patriotic pail

Rejuvenate an old bucket by wrapping it in the colors of the American flag.

total cost

pail	$1.00
rope	5.99
total	**$6.99**

what you'll need
Metal pail with handle
Hot-glue gun and glue sticks
4 yards of ¼-inch-diameter red, white, and blue striped rope
Scissors

here's how
1 Wash and dry the pail.
2 Starting at the bottom of the pail, hot-glue the end of the rope to the pail. Working with small sections at a time, tightly wrap the rope around the pail and glue it in place. When you reach the top of the pail, wrap the handle with rope.
3 Continue gluing the rope down the side of the pail. Cut off the excess rope. If desired, glue rope down on the opposite side of the pail. Secure the ends with glue if needed.

(86) star paperweights

Embedded with gems, beads, and swirls of solder, these paperweights sparkle with the red, white, and blue.

what you'll need
Star-shape cookie cutter; waxed paper
Permanent marking pen; scissors
Disposable bowl; plaster of Paris; plastic knife
Lead-free solder in silver, red, blue, and clear; wire cutters; gems; eyelets; beads
Thick white crafts glue; paintbrush
Glitter in silver, red, or blue

total cost

cookie cutter	$1.29
marking pen	1.59
plaster of Paris	.79
trims	2.29
glitter	.69
total	$6.65

here's how
1 Trace around the cookie cutter on waxed paper with marking pen. Cut out the shape ½ inch beyond marking.
2 Press the waxed paper shape into the cookie cutter, letting it fold up the sides.
3 In a disposable bowl mix plaster of Paris according to the manufacturer's directions. Carefully pour the plaster into the lined cookie cutter, filling it three-quarters full. Smooth off with a plastic knife.
4 To make a solder coil, cut a short piece and form it into a coil. Place a bend approximately ¼ inch from one end. Press this end into the plaster.
5 Press the remaining embellishments into the wet plaster where desired. Let the plaster dry.
6 Remove the star shape from the cookie cutter. Remove the waxed paper. Paint a coat of glue on the edges of the star shape. Sprinkle the wet glue with glitter. Let dry.

(87) wood stars

Stack sanded wood stars to make rustic votive candleholders that are full of spirit.

what you'll need
Tracing paper; pencil
Star-shape cookie cutters in two sizes, optional
Scissors
Various thicknesses of wood
Scroll saw or jigsaw
Drill and 1½-inch bit
Acrylic paints in blue, red, and yellow
Paintbrush
Sandpaper
Wood glue
Tea light candle

here's how
1 On tracing paper, draw star patterns or trace around cookie cutters; cut out. For a set of three candleholders, trace around each pattern three times on wood. Cut out pieces using a scroll saw or jigsaw.
2 Carefully drill holes ¼ inch deep in the centers of the smaller stars. Paint the stars the desired color. Let dry. Sand off the paint around the edges.
3 Glue the smaller star onto the larger star. Let dry. Place a tea light in the hole.

Note: Never leave burning candles unattended.

total cost

wood	$1.50
paints	2.89
tea light candle	.25
total	$4.64

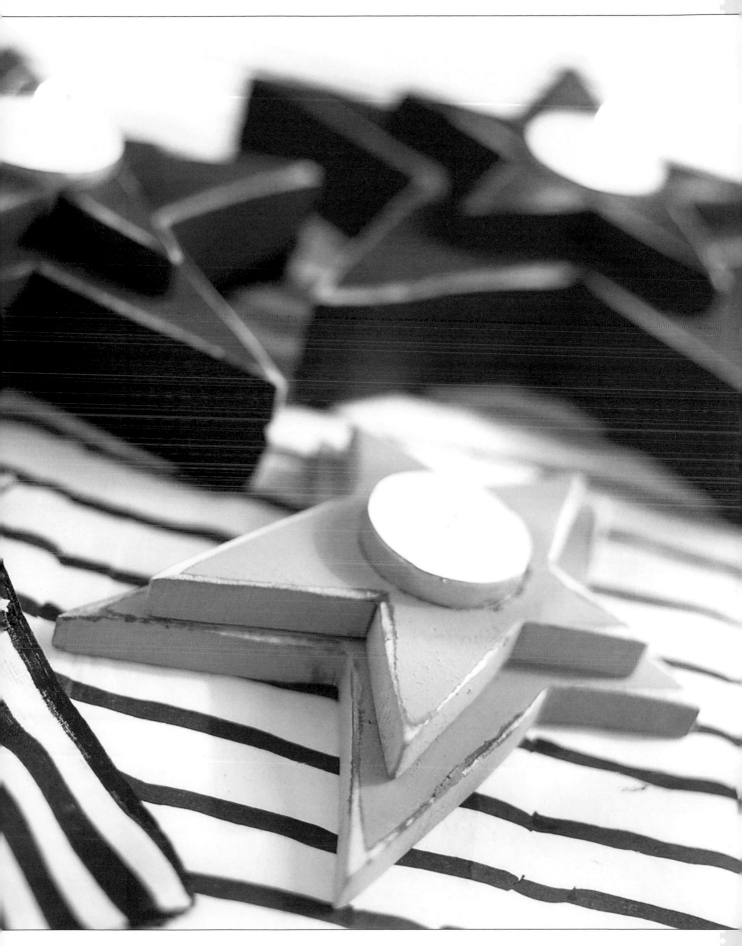

(88) all-american plate

Show your American pride by making and displaying this grand plate.

what you'll need
Glass plate; newspapers
Krylon Looking Glass mirror spray paint and clear-coat sealer, such as Metalcast (available at car supply stores)
Tube-style fabric paint; scissors
Adhesive-back paper
Crafts knife
Transparent spray paints, such as Dupli-Color, in red and blue
Felt; pen; thick white crafts glue

here's how
1 Wash and dry the plate. On newspaper in a well-ventilated work area, spray the back of the plate with three to four light coats of mirror spray paint, letting dry between coats. Spray sealer over the painted area. Let dry.
2 Write lettering on the front of the plate with tube-style fabric paint. Let dry.
3 Cut star and lines from adhesive-back paper. Place on plate front below lettering as shown in photo, *above.*
4 Spray the front side of the plate with red from one edge, bleeding off into the center. Spray blue beginning at opposite side, bleeding into center, overlapping slightly onto red. Let dry.
5 Carefully remove star and adhesive-back paper and peel away lettering.
6 Trace around plate bottom on felt and trim slightly smaller than drawn line. Cut out the felt. Glue felt to the back of plate.

total cost

plate	$1.50
paints and sealer	5.88
felt	.25
paper	.40
total	$8.03

89 star-studded candle

Edge a candle with metallic gold stars and chain to shimmer in the light of the flame.

what you'll need
Tape measure; red 3-wick candle
7 metallic gold upholstery tacks
18 inches of jewelry chain
7 metallic gold star charms

here's how
1 Measure the circumference of the candle and divide the measurement by 7.
2 Use a tack to make a tiny guide hole for each star at intervals determined in Step 1, approximately ¾ inch from candle top.
3 Push a tack through the end link of the chain and then through a charm loop. Press the tack into one of the guide holes in the candle. Continue tacking the charms and chain in place, allowing the chain to create scallops between the tacks.

Note: Never leave burning candles unattended.

total cost

candle	$3.59
tacks	.42
chain	.89
charms	3.50
total	$8.40

jam 'n' jelly jar tags

(90)

Accompany a gift from the kitchen with a pretty cut-paper tag.

what you'll need

Heavyweight paper or tagboard; ruler
Straight or decorative-edge scissors
Brush pen in desired color
Metallic gold permanent marking pen
1½×2¾-inch white adhesive label
⅛-inch paper punch
12 inches of metallic gold elastic cord

here's how

1 Cut the heavyweight paper into a 3½×1½-inch strip using straight or decorative-edge scissors. If desired, cut off the corners of the paper strip.

2 Color the paper strip using a brush pen. Carefully outline the edges of the paper strip using a gold marking pen. Outline the adhesive label with gold marking pen. Center the label on the cut strip of paper and press into place.

3 Punch a small hole in each end of the tag. Cut a 12-inch length of cord. Thread the cord through the holes; tie around jar.

total cost

paper scraps for five tags	$ .50
brush pen	1.89
marking pen	.99
label	.05
cord	.10
total	**$3.53**

⟨91⟩ denim carryall

Accented with trims from the hardware store, this fashionable purse is made from the leg of an old pair of jeans.

total cost

washers	$1.06
jewelry glue	1.29
chain	2.79
closures	.50
total	$5.64

what you'll need

Old jeans; scissors; ruler; sewing machine; thread
Approximately 32—³⁄₁₆-inch washers
Jewelry glue; pliers
2 feet of twisted nickel chain; carpet thread; needle
Two ³⁄₄-inch-diameter circular closures, such as Velcro

here's how

1 Cut 9½ inches off the end of one jean leg. If the hem is frayed, cut it off and turn the edge over to the front, turning under the raw edge. Stitch.
2 Turn the jean leg wrong side out. Line up the outside and inside seams so they run down the center. Stitch across the bottom cut edge using a ¼-inch seam. Clip the corners and turn right side out.
3 Glue washers in offset rows on the front of the purse.
4 Open the last links on each end of the chain and slip a washer on each link. Pinch the link closed. Hand-stitch washers to the top corners of the purse with carpet thread.
5 Glue closures to the inside edges of the purse.

⚬92⚬ charming chains

Hit the toolbox, not your jewelry box, the next time you need to jazz up an outfit with some dangling chains.

what you'll need
20-inch-long board; 2 nails; ruler; hammer
15-foot-long piece of bathtub chain; scissors
Wire cutters; masking tape; fishing line
2 silver cap beads; 2 silver flat beads; 2 silver round beads; 24 inches of narrow black cord
Thick white crafts glue; 2 small silver beads

total cost

chain	$2.18
fishing line	.10
beads	1.66
cord	.10
total	$4.04

here's how
1 On the board, pound two nails 18 inches apart.
2 Cut length of chain into two equal pieces. Tape the end of one piece to the end of the board near one nail. Wind chain around nails to create loops. Tape the end of the chain to the board. Repeat for second piece of chain.
3 Tie an 18-inch piece of fishing line around loops of chain at each nail. Make a double knot. Remove tape and slip loops off nails, allowing ends to dangle. Thread a cap bead onto fishing line at each end of necklace and double-knot the fishing line.
4 Thread a flat bead and then a round bead onto the fishing line. Slip both ends of the fishing line back through the round bead only, leaving two loops of fishing line at the top of the bead. Repeat for the other necklace end.
5 Cut black cord in half; knot one end of each cord. Slip knotted end through the fishing line loop. Pull loose ends of fishing line to close loop around knotted cord. Thread line through flat bead; tie line into a double knot under the flat bead. Apply glue to knot; cut off excess line. Repeat for other end.
6 Add small silver bead to end of each cord; knot. Gather four loose strands of chain; tie together in an overhand knot centered in the other chain loops.

(93) stepping-stone

Use your imagination to create a stepping-stone for your backyard oasis.

what you'll need
Plastic tub for mixing
Trowel
Cement mix
10-inch-diameter disposable round plastic planter tray
One 2⅝-inch square green tile
4 tiny terra-cotta flowerpots
4 iridescent purple marbles
Fourteen 1⅜-inch square red tiles
Large spoon
Brown sand

here's how
1 In the plastic tub, mix the cement with the trowel using small amounts of cement mix and water. It should be the consistency of a pourable dough, thin enough to pour slowly without running from the container. Mix a little more than what you think you need.
2 Pour the cement into the planter tray, filling it to the top. Shake the tray from side to side and tap firmly to settle the cement. Smooth the surface with the trowel.
3 Place items in cement in desired arrangement. Tap the items with the back of a spoon until they are firmly in place and settled to the desired depth. For container items, such as the tiny terra-cotta pots, spoon cement into the hollowed portion to stabilize the piece.
4 Pour sand on top of wet cement, covering the entire stone.
5 Leave stone stationary for 24 hours. Let it dry. Pour off the excess sand and wash off any remaining cement from embedded items, wiping with dry cloth. Gently turn stone over to remove it from the tray.

total cost

cement	$2.49
planter tray	.39
tiles	4.35
flowerpots	1.16
marbles	.20
sand	.50
total	$9.09

fruited vinegar bottle

94

Unexpected materials enhance an unassuming bottle, transforming it into a kitchen treasure.

what you'll need
Plastic net bag (from grocery store produce)
Bottle with cork
Glue gun and low-melt glue
Artificial fruit
12 inches of metallic gold cord

here's how
1 Slip the plastic net bag over the bottle. Use low-melt glue and a glue gun to glue the net to the bottom of the bottle. Let the glue dry. Tie the netting around the neck of the bottle.
2 Wrap and bend a stem of fruit and leaves around the neck of the bottle. Tie gold cord around the neck. Knot cord ends.

total cost

bottle	$1.29
artificial fruit	.79
cord	.10
total	$2.18

(95) sunshine bowls

Turn any meal into a celebration by presenting summer's best in bowls wrapped in bright papers.

what you'll need
Newspapers; wood bowl (available in thrift shops)
White spray primer
Acrylic paint in desired color
Paintbrush
Papers in several colors
Scissors; paper punch
Decoupage medium, such as Mod Podge
Glass or plastic liner, optional

here's how
1 In a well-ventilated work area, cover work surface with newspapers. Spray bowl with primer. Let dry. Paint the bowl the desired color. Let dry.
2 Cut paper strips and squares. Punch circles with a paper punch. Paint decoupage medium onto the bowl and arrange the paper shapes on the bowl. Paint two more coats of decoupage medium over the bowl. Let it dry.
3 Place a glass or plastic liner in the bowl if using it for food.

total cost

bowl	$1.69
primer	1.89
paint	1.29
papers	.40
total	$5.27

fingerprint
fish clock

Blend paint with your fingertips and press onto a clock frame to make a school of delightful fish.

what you'll need
Disposable plate
Acrylic paints in desired colors
Clock with frame
Fine paintbrush

here's how
1 Place small amounts of paint on a disposable plate. To make fish bodies, dip fingers and thumb into paints, blending colors if desired. Press fingers and thumb onto surface of clock frame as shown in the photo, *opposite.* Continue making fingerprints on the clock frame until approximately two-thirds of the frame is covered. Let the paint dry.
2 Paint details on the fish, such as fins, eyes, and smiles, using desired colors of paint and a fine paintbrush. Let the paint dry.

total cost

paints	$2.30
clock	4.00
total	$6.30

97 true-colors plates

Show your love of country with these recycled-license-plate flags.

total cost

primer	$2.59
paints	2.50
sealer	2.39
wire	.40
dowel	.79
stencil	.99
total	**$9.66**

what you'll need
Sandpaper
Old license plate
Soft cloth; newspapers; white spray primer
Acrylic paints in navy, red, and white; paintbrush
Star stencil
Matte clear acrylic sealer
Drill and bit; 20-gauge wire; wire cutters
24-inch-long piece of ⅜-inch dowel; pencil

here's how
1 Lightly sand front of license plate. Wipe clean with soft cloth.
2 In a well-ventilated work area, cover work surface with newspapers. Spray the plate with white primer. Let dry.
3 Paint various flag patterns as shown, *below*. Use star stencil to paint stars. Let dry.
4 Spray the plate with acrylic sealer.
5 Drill holes in the plate and dowel. Wire the plate to the dowel, leaving long ends. Curl the wire ends by wrapping several times around a pencil.

(98) sand candles

With just a few supplies and a couple of quick steps, you can create tiny candleholders for each of your picnic guests.

what you'll need
Glass salt and pepper shakers
Colored sand
Glass adhesive
Small candles

hero's how
1 Fill the salt and pepper shakers with colored sand.
2 To stack shakers, adhere together using glass adhesive. Let the adhesive dry.
3 Place a candle in the top of each holder.

Note: Never leave burning candles unattended.

total cost

salt and pepper shaker set	$3.29
sand	2.79
candles	.60
total	$6.68

⑨⑨ blue ribbon jelly jars

Be a winner all year long with canning jars trimmed with artificial fruits and vegetables.

what you'll need
Artificial fruits or vegetables
Additional canning jar lid
Thick white crafts glue
Jar filled with canned fruit or vegetables

here's how
1 Glue artificial fruits or vegetables to the top of an extra canning jar lid and allow the glue to dry.
2 Glue the topper to the lid of your canned produce, gluing to the rim of the lid. Remove the topper before opening the jar.

total cost

artificial fruit or vegetables	$ .89
lid	.20
jar	1.00
total	$2.09

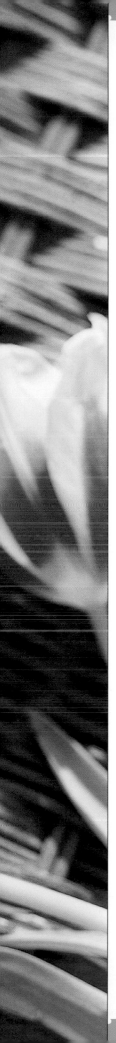

gardentime tools

100

Enjoy planting time using garden tools with hand-wrapped seed-packet handles.

what you'll need
Empty seed packets
Pinking shears
Garden tool
Thick white crafts glue; paintbrush
Scraps of 1-inch-wide grosgrain ribbon; pencil
Scissors
Scraps of narrow ribbon or rickrack

here's how
1 Cut out the front of seed packets using pinking shears. Arrange on tool handle as desired, allowing 1 inch at the top and bottom for ribbon. Glue in place using water-thinned crafts glue. Let dry.
2 Apply two coats of thinned glue over seed packets, allowing to dry between coats.
3 Trace around end of tool handle on 1-inch-wide grosgrain ribbon. Cut out circle. Glue to end of handle using crafts glue. Glue short lengths of ribbon at the top and bottom of the handle. Let dry.
4 Glue short lengths of narrow ribbon or rickrack over the grosgrain ribbon. Let dry.
5 Coat the entire handle with thinned glue. Let dry.

total cost

garden tool	$2.49
ribbon and rickrack	1.25
total	$3.74

index

sources & credits

Adhesives

Aleenes
duncancrafts.com

Centis
Centis Consumer Products
Division
888/236-8476

Elmer's Glue Stick
800/848-9400
elmers.com
comments@elmers.com

Beads

The Beadery
105 Canonchet Rd.
Hope Valley, RI 02832
thebeadery.com

Felt

National Nonwovens
P.O. Box 150
Easthampton, MA 01027

Notions

Collins & Omnigrid, Inc.
Prym-Dritz Corporation
P.O. Box 5028
Spartanburg, SC 29304
dritz.com

Opaque Writers & Waterproof Markers

EK Success Ltd.
eksuccess.com
(Wholesale only. Available at most
crafts supply stores.)

Papers

Paper Adventures
P.O. Box 04393
Milwaukee, WI 53204
paperadventures.com

Scissors & Punches

Fiskars Brands, Inc.
608/259-1649
fiskars.com

EK Success Ltd.
eksuccess.com
(Wholesale only. Available at most
crafts supply stores.)

Ribbon

Midori
708 6th Ave. N
Seattle, WA 98109
midoriribbon.com

Silk Ribbon

YLI Corporation
161 West Main St.
Rock Hill, SC 29730

Bucilla
3225 Westech Dr.
Norcross, GA 30092
plaidonline.com

Snowman Cake Pan

Wilton Enterprises
2240 West 75th St.
Woodridge, IL 60517
wilton.com

Designers
Susan Banker
Heidi Boyd
Carol Field Dahlstrom
Phyllis Dunstan
Donna Chesnut
Sandi Jorgensen
Carol Linnan
Ginny McKeever
Margaret Sindelar
Alice Wetzel

Photography
Photographers
Peter Krumhardt
Scott Little
Andy Lyons Cameraworks

Photostyling
Carol Field Dahlstrom
Margaret Sindelar
Judy Bailey, assistant
Donna Chesnut, assistant